CAMBRIDGE LIBRARY COLLECTION

Books of enduring scholarly value

Linguistics

From the earliest surviving glossaries and translations to nineteenth century academic philology and the growth of linguistics during the twentieth century, language has been the subject both of scholarly investigation and of practical handbooks produced for the upwardly mobile, as well as for travellers, traders, soldiers, missionaries and explorers. This collection will reissue a wide range of texts pertaining to language, including the work of Latin grammarians, groundbreaking early publications in Indo-European studies, accounts of indigenous languages, many of them now extinct, and texts by pioneering figures such as Jacob Grimm, Wilhelm von Humboldt and Ferdinand de Saussure.

Lectures upon the Assyrian Language and Syllabary

Archibald Henry Sayce (1845–1933) became interested in Middle Eastern languages and scripts while still a teenager. Old Persian and Akkadian cuneiform had recently been deciphered, and popular enthusiasm for these discoveries was running high when Sayce began his academic career at Oxford in 1869. He had already published two grammars of Assyrian (both reissued in this series) by the time these lively and engaging lectures, given in 1875 and 1876, were published in 1877. The introduction expresses optimism that Assyrian and Egyptian would establish themselves as core components of the university curriculum alongside Greek and Hebrew. Acknowledging the 'repellent difficulties' of learning the Assyrian syllabary, Sayce devotes three lectures to discussing the building blocks of this ancient mode of writing. He then addresses the phonology, pronouns, verbs and syntax of the language. The last of his nine lectures considers the place of Assyrian within the Semitic language family.

T0382504

Cambridge University Press has long been a pioneer in the reissuing of out-of-print titles from its own backlist, producing digital reprints of books that are still sought after by scholars and students but could not be reprinted economically using traditional technology. The Cambridge Library Collection extends this activity to a wider range of books which are still of importance to researchers and professionals, either for the source material they contain, or as landmarks in the history of their academic discipline.

Drawing from the world-renowned collections in the Cambridge University Library and other partner libraries, and guided by the advice of experts in each subject area, Cambridge University Press is using state-of-the-art scanning machines in its own Printing House to capture the content of each book selected for inclusion. The files are processed to give a consistently clear, crisp image, and the books finished to the high quality standard for which the Press is recognised around the world. The latest print-on-demand technology ensures that the books will remain available indefinitely, and that orders for single or multiple copies can quickly be supplied.

The Cambridge Library Collection brings back to life books of enduring scholarly value (including out-of-copyright works originally issued by other publishers) across a wide range of disciplines in the humanities and social sciences and in science and technology.

Lectures upon the
Assyrian Language and Syllabary

Delivered to Students of the Archaic Classes

Archibald Henry Sayce

CAMBRIDGE
UNIVERSITY PRESS

University Printing House, Cambridge, CB2 8BS, United Kingdom

Cambridge University Press is part of the University of Cambridge.

It furthers the University's mission by disseminating knowledge in the pursuit of
education, learning and research at the highest international levels of excellence.

www.cambridge.org
Information on this title: www.cambridge.org/9781108077750

© in this compilation Cambridge University Press 2014

This edition first published 1877
This digitally printed version 2014

ISBN 978-1-108-07775-0 Paperback

LECTURES

UPON

THE ASSYRIAN LANGUAGE,

AND

SYLLABARY.

LECTURES

UPON THE

ASSYRIAN LANGUAGE,

AND

SYLLABARY;

DELIVERED TO

THE STUDENTS OF THE ARCHAIC CLASSES.

BY

REV. A. H. SAYCE, M.A.,

Deputy Professor of Comparative Philology, Oxford.

Multæ terricolis linguæ, cœlestibus una.

LONDON:

SAMUEL BAGSTER AND SONS,

15, PATERNOSTER ROW.

1877.

CONTENTS.

———

PREFACE.

THE following Lectures form part of an experiment which took practical shape through the unwearied exertions of Mr. W. R. Cooper, the Secretary of the Society of Biblical Archæology. Classes in Egyptian and Assyrian were started in the rooms of the Society in the spring of 1875; Mr. Le Page Renouf superintending the first, and myself the second. The three first Lectures on the syllabary embody the substance of the Lectures delivered in 1875, before an audience which averaged some thirty students; the remaining Lectures occupied the spring of 1876, the second year of the experiment. The success which attended it leads to the hope that English schools of Egyptology and Assyriology may be permanently formed, and the study of the monumental languages of the great nations of antiquity placed on the same footing as the study of Hebrew.

For Assyrian, two classes of students are urgently required. One, whose eyesight and practice shall enable them to copy the minute characters of the Assyrian tablets with photographic accuracy; the other, who shall bring to the task of decipherment all the varied stores of Semitic philology and learning. Of course both classes must, to a certain extent, intermingle their acquirements; the philologist ought to be able to control the epigraphist, and the epigraphist to have some knowledge of Semitic philology. But in these days of divided labour, and in a subject of so vast extent as Assyrian decipherment, it is not necessary, indeed it is rarely possible, that the two specialties should be united in the same person. Ordinarily, the philologist must content himself merely with that knowledge of epigraphy needful for his purpose, the epigraphist with that knowledge of philology needful to guide him in his readings. Inasmuch, however, as the study of Assyrian is a monumental one, the philologist will have to be an epigraphist to a far greater extent than is the case with the classical scholar.

There is no doubt a good deal in the following Lectures which may have to be corrected by subsequent discovery. Such must always be the case with a progressive study. Nevertheless, the main outlines of Assyrian grammar have now been sketched with clearness and certainty, its main problems have been solved, and the details alone left to be filled in. I, for one, believe that the day is not far distant when it will be recognised that a knowledge of Assyrian is as important for comparative Semitic philology as is a knowledge of Sanskrit for the comparative study of the Aryan languages.

A. H. SAYCE.

Queen's College, Oxford, June 6th, 1877.

PHILOLOGICAL LECTURES

ON THE

ASSYRIAN LANGUAGE.

LECTURE I.

On the Study of the Assyrian Language.

IT is with mingled feelings of gratification and diffidence that I come before you this evening to open a series of lectures, the character and object of which are new and even revolutionary in the history of our studies and education. For the first time in this country an attempt will be made to found a system of instruction in languages, which it has been the glory of the present century to recover from the past, which are clothed with all the modern interest that attaches to the great problems of the development of civilization, and which demand, not mere memory or dependence upon the authority of others, but the new methods of patient scientific induction. Thanks to the exertions of the indefatigable Secretary of the *Society of Biblical Archæology*, Mr. W. R. Cooper, my colleague Mr. Le Page Renouf and myself are enabled to bring before your notice classics more ancient than those of Greece or Rome, or even Judea—classics, too, which are written on contemporaneous monuments, and must be spelled out, as it were, from the lips of a living people—explaining the details of their grammar and idioms, and the key which has unlocked their secrets. The knowledge of all this has hitherto been confined, like the sacred learning of Egyptian priests, to a small band of workers, from whom the world has been content to accept the startling results which have from time to time awakened its incredulity or excited its interest; and no endeavour has yet been made in England to bring the languages and the literature of the pioneers of civilization out of the mysterious shadow-land of the specialist into the commonplace light of the lecture-room and the school. Shall I be considered presumptuous if I say that the courses of lectures which I have been permitted to inaugurate this evening mark an era in national education? I cannot express the gratification I feel at the attendance which I see before me, so large beyond my boldest expectations, and so encouraging to the success of our work. A few years back the languages and the literature, which will be the subject of our studies, lay forgotten and unknown under the rubbish of centuries, or in the dusty corners of European museums; still fewer years ago they were but a sealed book to all but one or two daring scholars who alone were attempting to penetrate their contents. Already they stand on a level with the manifold subjects of human know-ledge which are taught and learned, and the students who have gathered this evening to help us in founding schools and educational courses of Assyrian and Egyptian philology, are a token that a fresh start has been made in the education of the country, and a fresh realm of conquest opened out before the mind.

For, we must remember, the study of Assyrian and Egyptian philology differs in several very essential points from the studies with which we are usually familiar; and since the method by which it must be learnt is a new one, a new method also must be devised for teaching it. Firstly, and especially, the teacher and the pupil must both alike be learners, and the difference between them is one of degree only, and not of kind. The teacher is but a little in advance of the pupil, but feeling a way, as it were, for the latter, and even in the act of teaching, is making fresh discoveries, and rectifying old conclusions. There is no authoritative standard to be referred to, no tradition to be appealed to, no dictionary to be consulted; all must be worked out by the laborious comparison of texts, by extensive knowledge of cognate languages, by ready combination and hypothesis, and by the trained judgment of scientific research. In short, the decipherer is as much a discoverer as the man of science, the chief distinction between them being, that whereas the man of science has now a tradition, an authority, a standard to look up to, the decipherer is still engaged in creating one, and elaborating out of his own experience a method for others to follow. Such a pursuit is thoroughly in harmony with the independent and inquiring spirit of our own age—indeed, we can hardly imagine it arising at any previous period; and the work we have before us is none other than to cast into what we may call an educational mould this embodiment of our nineteenth century spirit. It is to do for language and literature, for *litteræ humaniores*, in fact, what was done two or three centuries ago for science. Such an attempt has perhaps never been made before, unless we go back to the time when Athenian sophists and orators were struggling to find out the force and meaning of the words they uttered and framing a Greek Grammar. Since then the literary and linguistic education of Europe has been confined within the limits of a traditional system. The Romans made Greek the basis of instruction, and so built up a grammar and literature of their own, which have formed the groundwork and staple of the education of later times. There have always been a framework and method to fall back upon, accidentally in existence if you like, but still in existence it was; and the young mind was accordingly kept in the leading-strings of the past, and taught to lean upon a cramping authority. To feel and exert its own powers, to educate itself in the truest and fullest sense of the word, is a task that has been reserved for our own days. In the decipherment of the ancient classics of Babylon and Egypt, in the gradual recovery of that Oriental past, which is so all-important for the history of intellectual development, as much as in discoveries of science, the servant is not above his master; and the reason is the same in each case, for the method which we have to employ is no less the comparative method of inductive science than that of the chemist or geologist.

The second point in which the subject of our lectures differs widely from the subjects of the ordinary curriculum, is its contemporaneous character. We have not to deal with the late MS. copies of illiterate or careless scribes, but with the very documents which came from their authors' hands. It is true that many of these are copies or editions of older records, so that the purity of the text may still exercise the intelligence and call forth the reasoning powers of the scholar; but, nevertheless, they were written when the language was yet living and spoken, and their very faults are a valuable evidence of the state of the language and its speakers at the time they were inscribed. Epigraphy is one of the studies which has grown up of late years, and from the nature of things it must always take but a subordinate place in the study of Latin and Greek; but epigraphy, in the sense of the study of contemporaneous records, is the sum and substance of our Assyrian and Egyptian researches, which are essentially occupied with the decipherment of contemporaneous *inscriptions*. This contemporaneousness is of inestimable importance, even from an educational point of view. To find oneself face to face with the writers we study, to reach them through no later channels, more or less fallacious, but to speak to them as to living men, removes that artificial unreality which as those who have had anything to do with education know too well exercises so fatal and dulling an influence upon the mind. From other points of view besides the purely educational one, the manifold advantages that result from having to deal with contemporaneous documents need not be dwelt upon. One only will I single out, as that has a special bearing upon the immediate subject of these lectures. I mean the opportunity thus afforded us of tracing the growth and history of the language from the period when it first becomes literary, down to its closing epoch. It is only in this way that we can ever really come to know a language, and the certainty with which we can do so in Assyrian makes the latter invaluable not only for Semitic philology in particular, but for comparative philology in general. Already, as will be noted in the course of these lectures, light has been thrown by Assyrian upon some of the obscurest points of Semitic grammar, while the discovery of Accadian, the oldest form of agglutinative speech, is likely to create a revolution in Turanian studies, and to solve not a few of the problems of the science of language. Elucidation of Semitic philology necessarily brings with it elucidation of the Old Testament writings; and questions like that of the possibility of a Hebrew construction, or the probability of a corrupt reading, can only be decided by monuments inscribed in a kindred dialect at a time when Hebrew was still a spoken tongue.

The third and last point to which I shall advert wherein these lectures and classes are introducing a new educational force, is their testimony that there is something worth learning besides the time-honoured subjects of school and University training. We are apt to become narrow and conventional in our habits of thought, and to regard everything with which we are unfamiliar as barbarian. It is the old error of the Greek and Roman over again. We must learn that there was a culture and civilization five or six thousand years ago on the banks of the Nile and Euphrates which would compare favourably with that of our forefathers but three or four centuries since, and that the literary productions of these ancient people are as admirable *in their own way* as the masterpieces which have stereotyped our canons of taste. The merits of this or that study, of this or that method of education, are but relative ; and it may yet turn out that a study and method which require the free and unchecked exercise of our mental powers, which demand all the qualities on which the man of science prides himself, and which call us back to originals rather than to copies, are more in harmony with the needs of a future generation than the studies and the methods which now possess our minds.

There is one fact, however, which must not be blinked, and it is a fact that meets us on the very threshold of our researches. The languages we propose to study are concealed and buried beneath a pyramid of strange and uncouth characters. Before proceeding a single step, we have to load our memories with an endless and intricate syllabary. The preliminary toil is very great, and it is well that this should be realised at the outset. But let us remember that nothing good and sound has ever been achieved without trouble, and that if we mean serious work we cannot expect to find everything smooth and easy-going. The life of the scholar and the life of the *dilettante* are two very different things ; but the *dilettante* never accomplishes anything except the selfish art of killing time. Do not, then, be frightened by the multitude of polyphonous characters which have to be learned before we can interpret the Assyrian inscriptions to any purpose, or the long lists of hieroglyphics which Mr. Le Page Renouf will require you to commit to memory. These diffi-culties have been overcome by others before you, and a time will come when the acquisition of a new character will bring with it a real pleasure. But let us not be deceived into thinking that we can study Assyrian and Egyptian without first mastering the characters in which these languages are written. Transliteration may be a good help, but it will be a broken reed to lean upon alone. Confining myself to Assyrian I must recall the fact that the existence of polyphones necessitates a combination of the decipherer and philologist.

We cannot speculate on the meaning and affinities of a word unless we know
how to read it, and we cannot know how to read it unless we also know what
value to select in any given case out of the many possible ones a character
may bear. All that I can do is to lighten the burden of learning this ponderous
syllabary by explaining its origin, and setting forth the rules to be followed in
reading the inscriptions; and this I shall try to do in the first two or three
lectures. But I cannot prevent the task from being a distasteful and irksome
one, and from having perforce to be gone through.

There is yet another point on which I would remove all chances of a false
impression. Just as the preliminary labour of learning the syllabary must be
no holiday amusement, so also must the study of the Assyrian grammar
be thoroughgoing and scholarly. We must have no slovenly and merely
approximate translations; and while in the course of these lectures I shall
keep your attention fixed upon the principal outlines and main facts of the
Assyrian grammar, I shall at the same time insist upon those small niceties
and distinctions which are apt to be overlooked by the hasty and superficial
student, but which stamp and distinguish a language more than anything else,
and prevent the translator from losing the idiom, and with that the sense and
meaning of the original. It will often be found that the signification of
important passages depends upon this accuracy of scholarship. In a Semitic
language it is the verb in which these niceties are liable to be ridden roughshod
over, to the detriment not only of the study of the language itself, but even
more of the force and drift of the text. The conception which underlies the
Semitic verb is so radically different from that to which we are accustomed in
our own family of speech, that careful investigation alone can really discover
its various forms and uses. It is only within the present century that any true
knowledge of the Hebrew verb has been arrived at, and passages of the Old
Testament, which before seemed hopelessly obscure, cleared up and assigned
their true meaning. By way of illustration, take, for instance, the first few
verses of Genesis. We all know well the way in which they are translated in
our authorised version. But when we give each of the tenses employed in them
the peculiar force and signification which modern research has shown them to
have, ascribing to the perfect בָּרָא its sense of completion, to the perfect,
divided from the copula by the subject, its pluperfect value, to the participle
its meaning of continuance, to the imperfect with *waw consecutive* its sense of

subordination and incipiency, what a change is made in the meaning of the whole passage, what fresh vividness is given to the picture! " In the beginning God hewed out the heaven and the earth: now the earth had been waste and desolate, and darkness on the face of the deep; and the Spirit of God was ever brooding on the face of the waters; and God said," etc. Here a new signification has been put into the verses by modern research—a new life breathed into them by a more accurate knowledge of the Hebrew verb. Now, just as we cannot afford to study Hebrew without thoroughly acquainting ourselves with its use of the tenses, so also ought it to be in Assyrian. Merely to be able to give a sort of rough guess at the signification of a sentence, setting down what we believe to be the substance of it, and overlooking all the finer points of grammatical idiom, is not to be a translator in the proper sense of the word. Before everything else, grammatical accuracy is absolutely requisite. When once we are sure of the grammar of a passage, the lexical difficulties will soon disappear. Of course this close attention to what has been contemptuously termed " the minutiæ of Assyrian grammar," is not likely to be popular. But again, let us remind ourselves that we are here not to be *dilettanti*, but scholars. Following the late Dr. Hincks, I have stood almost alone in the endeavour to trace the meanings and usages of different forms of the Assyrian verb, protesting against the rough-and-ready process that would lump them all together indiscriminately, and place Assyrian grammar on the same footing as was Hebrew grammar before the investigations of modern scholars. My *Assyrian Grammar* was an attempt, however inadequate and humble, to do for Assyrian what Ewald or Olshausen have done for Hebrew; and I am glad to think that the attempt has not been altogether a failure. One by one my colleagues in the study of Assyrian have adopted my views, at all events in principle; and my friend, Dr. Schrader, who once expressed his unqualified and emphatic dissent from them, has so far come to agree with me that he acknowledges the difference between us to be now one of name only. The system of grammar propounded in the present lectures will be in accordance with the principles laid down in my " Grammar." Much that I have said there was polemical, and now therefore superfluous, while, in some other respects, it has had to be supplemented or modified; it will, therefore, be the substance of my maturer conclusions, based upon a fuller investigation of the inscriptions, which will be given in the lectures it is my privilege to deliver before you. You will, I think, be convinced that the subtle and extensive machinery of the Assyrian verb, so far from being one to make " Semitic philologists shake the head," is in full harmony with that of Hebrew or Ethiopic or Arabic, and the surest token which we possess of the pure Semitism of the Assyrian tongue. The perfection is only what we should expect from a language so complete and primitive in character and age, and throws a flood of light upon a long misunderstood part of Semitic philology.

LECTURE II.

The Syllabary.

———

A T the very threshold of his Assyrian studies the beginner is met by the most repulsive, but, nevertheless, an indispensable part of what he has to learn. Nothing is harder than to familiarise oneself with a new character which has not been learnt in childhood, and so become, as it were, part of the furniture of the mind. One's own language looks strange and difficult when written in a foreign alphabet, and even a page of the " Fonetic Nuz" requires some spelling out. But the repellent difficulties encountered in acquiring the knowledge of a new character are increased a thousandfold when the number of distinct characters amounts to four or five hundred, each of them possessing more than one value. Yet such is the case with the Assyrian syllabary; and it is well to state the full difficulties of it at once. The difficulties, however, will not prove insurmountable; and the best proof of the possibility of getting over them is that the powers of the numerous signs of the syllabary have all been made out one after the other by patient decipherers during the last twenty years, and that fresh scholars have from time to time been entering the field, undaunted by the task of mastering the Assyrian mode of writing. A Spanish author called his Basque Grammar " The Impossible Vanquished," and here we have to do with another " impossible " which can be vanquished with equal facility.

Now I cannot, of course, impress the Assyrian syllabary upon your memories, and make each character as familiar to you as the letters of our own alphabet without further trouble; but I can explain the way in which this cumbrous system of writing originated and grew up, and so (as I hope) can lighten your labours in learning it. The reason of a thing is more than half the whole; and when we are arrived at years of discretion, and have ceased to repeat our lessons by rote, like a cage of parrots, our memory is enormously aided by being accompanied by the intelligence. To understand is to remember.

What I shall try to do, therefore, in this second lecture, is to point out the basis and system upon which the Assyrian syllabary rests, or, in other words, to give a sketch of its origin and development. Before doing this, however, I would impress upon you the necessity of learning some portion at least of the syllabary before attempting to read the inscriptions. To depend upon the transliteration of another is always unsatisfactory; doubly so in the case of a syllabary, the characters of which have more than one value. If nothing more, at all events a knowledge sufficient to control the reading of an inscription is requisite. For merely comparative purposes, indeed, we may take on trust the transliterated examples of Assyrian grammatical forms; but if we want to translate the inscriptions for ourselves, and to enter into the niceties of the language, we *must* be able to read them as we would a work in Hebrew or Greek. It is not necessary to know all the characters of the syllabary and the manifold values of each; indeed, many of them are still unknown, and others occur only in a single passage, or in the bilingual tablets. But it *is* necessary to be acquainted with those in most frequent use, and the best preliminary to the study of Assyrian would be to learn as perfectly as possible the different characters and ideographs, with all their varying powers, which are prefixed to the first volume of Mr. Norris's dictionary. By going over them frequently, the eye would soon become habituated to their forms; and if, after gaining a first general knowledge of them the student would take some texts and endeavour to write these down in English letters, always keeping the syllabary at his side for reference, he would quickly find himself making astonishingly rapid advances. After a time, a complete syllabary like that given in my *Elementary Assyrian Grammar and Reading Book* (Bagster and Sons) should be used, and fresh signs and fresh values would thus be continually imprinting themselves upon the memory. Up to the last, however, he will discover that he cannot altogether dispense with such an aid, supplemented by himself, as it certainly will be, in the course of his own researches. It is happily not needful to burden the already over-weighted memory with the load of the whole Assyrian syllabary ; characters of rare occurrence can be hunted up whenever they are met with, and safely left to the keeping of a written memorandum. Even the Assyrian scribe of Assur-bani-pal's day, who had nothing else to occupy his thoughts, did not profess to recollect all the signs of his own system of writing. He sometimes, in copying, mistook characters of similar form for one another, and often came across a character stamped in the old style, of which he did not know the later equivalent ; while the best explanation that can be afforded of the fact that the syllabaria often give but a few out of the many values possessed by a particular character is that the writer could not remember at the time any more than those he has set down.[1] When there is so much that is important to remember, it is unwise to load our memories with what is needless. I do not think, however, that it is advisable to depend long upon texts already transliterated. No doubt it is useful at first to have an Assyrian character before you with the transliteration of it underneath ; but crutches of this kind should be thrown away as soon as possible. The requisite familiarity with the syllabary can never be acquired, so long as it is instinctively felt that help is close at hand without any trouble of thinking or searching for oneself ; we cannot be sure that we really know the power of a character if the eye can take in both the character and its power at a single glance. There will be a tendency, too, to take for granted the particular reading of the particular translator whose transliteration we are using, and prepossessions of this sort are among the hardest things to eradicate. A certain character (⊨⫿⌗) has, in Assyrian, the two common values of *saq* and *ris*, and when we meet with the word ⊨⫟ ⊨⫿⌗ ⊢⨳⫟ " oracle " we are likely to assume, without further question, that it must be read *pi-ris-tu* (from פרש) if Oppert has been the guide we have followed, and *pi-sak-tu* (from فستق) if Smith and Schrader have been the first to initiate us into the mysteries of Assyrian. The Assyrian student ought, above all things, to be independent, and it is only by mutual criticism that the interpretation of the inscriptions can progress. Transliterations of

---

[1] This of course does not exclude another fact which seems to account for the selected number of values assigned to a character in the syllabaria, namely that the scribe in compiling them went through some Accadian text, setting down those values, and those values only, which a particular character bore in that text.

texts are chiefly useful after an acquaintance with the syllabary has been assured. It saves time and trouble to be able to read off an inscription in a character less complicated than the Assyrian, and if we are thoroughly acquainted with the native characters, an error or uncertainty in the reading can be detected at once.

After these practical hints, we may now go on to the theoretical part of the subject. And the first question that starts up, strange as it may appear, is, what *is* the Assyrian syllabary which has to be learnt? Both the inscriptions and the printed texts offer us different types of writing, which seem to differ wholly from one another. We may be perfectly familiar with the inscriptions of Assur-bani-pal and yet utterly unable to make out those of Nebuchadrezzar; we may be able to read those legends of Sargon's which are lithographed in *Western Asiatic Inscriptions*, Vol. I., pl. 36, or Layard, pl. 33, and yet find ourselves hopelessly puzzled over the same monarch's inscription on the Cyprian monolith (*W. A. I.*, Vol. III., 11), or the obelisk of Samas-Rimmon; and a knowledge of all these may leave us uncertain of the values of the characters on the contract-stones of Babylonia, or the clay bricks of ancient Chaldea. Assyrian writing presents itself to us in at least four different forms, and sooner or later we shall have to acquire a certain amount of knowledge of all these four. First and foremost comes what we may call the *Archaic* form of writing, out of which the others have been gradually developed and simplified. The oldest inscriptions of which we know are written in the Archaic type, and they all come from the primitive cities of Chaldea. The numerous literary works copied and translated into Assyrian by order of Assur-bani-pal or his predecessors were originally inscribed in this style of cuneiform; and it occasionally happens that the original character is reproduced in the copy through the scribe's ignorance of its later Assyrian representative. A further development and simplification of this Archaic cuneiform is generally termed the *Hieratic*. The contract stones to which I alluded above may be said to be written in it; so also is the Cyprian inscription of Sargon and the obelisk records of Samas-Rimmon. Though a modification of the Archaic, it preserved the old forms of the characters much more closely than did the Assyrian, and was therefore used as a sort of black letter for ornamental purposes at the court of Nineveh. It is this use which has induced decipherers to call it Hieratic. Not very dissimilar to the Hieratic was the *Babylonian* cuneiform of Nebuchadrezzar and his cotemporaries; and the syllabary employed for the Assyrian transcripts of the Persian inscriptions at Behistun and elsewhere, as well as the selected syllabary of the Amardian or "Medo-Scythic" texts, is but a simplified edition of the Babylonian.[1] Distinct from all these, and simpler than any of them, except that of the Persian period, is the *Assyrian*, properly so called, which is found on the great mass of Assyrian monuments, from the sixteenth or fifteenth centuries B.C., down to the fall of the monarchy in the seventh. It is this kind of cuneiform which has been taken as the type and pattern of all the rest, and published in printed books. By far the largest part of the inscriptions we possess are written in it; and when we speak of learning the Assyrian syllabary, accordingly, we mean that syllabary which was specially and generally used in Assyria itself. After we have thoroughly learnt this syllabary, the other four styles of writing may be acquired without much additional labour: when once the *Assyrian* characters and their powers have been imprinted on the memory, a little care and patience will show the student how closely they are related to the corresponding Archaic, Hieratic, and Babylonian; how, indeed, their descent from these may in a certain sense be traced.

The cuneiform characters are degenerated hieroglyphics, like the Chinese symbols or the Demotic writing of ancient Egypt. A fragment of a tablet in the British Museum gives some of the primitive hieroglyphics side by side with the cuneiform characters which have been corrupted from them. Thus, the representation of a "comb" 𒀀 or 𒀀 is given as the original of 𒀀, Assyrian 𒀀. Difficult as it generally is to discover any likeness to a visible object in the signs of the Assyrian syllabary, we have often only to trace them back to their Archaic originals to see how a particular character came to stand for some particular object or idea. Primarily, therefore, every character denoted some object or conception; and we can thus understand how it came about that the characters of the Assyrian syllabary might be used as independent ideographs or hieroglyphics, as well

---

[1] In my Paper on the *Languages of the Cuneiform Inscriptions of Elam and Media*, in the *Transactions of the Society of Biblical Archæology*, Vol. III., 465-485, will be found reasons for the use of the term "Amardian." As "Protomedic," however, has now met with general acceptance, and is substantially correct, it will be employed throughout the rest of these Lectures.

as mere unmeaning syllabic sounds. If we could come across any specimens of the earliest attempts at writing in the Euphrates valley, we should expect to find them consisting altogether (or, at all events, for the most part) of ideographs; and, as a matter of fact, the brick legends of the Chaldean kings, as well as the old astrological tablets, contain many more ideographs than meaningless phonetic syllables. In the Assyrian period, on the other hand, the ideographic use of the characters was not common, except in special cases, and even here, as we shall see, phonetic complements were ordinarily added to them to show how they were to be read. In fact, such an ideographic use of the characters came to be mainly due to the desire of abbreviation, just as we write *viz.* for "namely," + for "plus," *i.e.* for "that is," and so forth. The clay tablets which served in the place of books were necessarily of small size, and this want of space will explain the continued employment of ideographs as well as the minuteness of the writing upon them. In the larger inscriptions on stone, the use of ideographs may be accounted for by the wish to end the line with the end of a word; and in this way ideographs in Assyrian played the part of *litteræ dilatabiles* in Hebrew. How long the primitive hieroglyphics took in passing into the cuneiform characters it is impossible to say. We shall see that there is good reason to suppose that writing on papyrus preceded writing on clay in Babylonia as well as in Egypt; and, while papyrus could be used for this purpose, there was nothing to prevent the original picture-writing from being preserved without corruption. With the introduction of the "burnt bricks" or *laterculæ coctiles*, as Pliny calls them, the case was altered. Angles had to supersede curves, circles to make way for straight lines. Picture-writing on any extended scale ceased to be possible; and the impress of the style upon the wet clay caused each line to assume a wedge-like form, the broad triangular base terminating in a thin point. We still possess specimens of writing in which the transition from the hieroglyphic to the cuneiform period is taking place. The hieroglyphics have ceased to be pictures, even more so than is the case with the Egyptian Hieratic, but the characteristic wedge has not yet appeared; the lines are still drawn of the same breadth throughout; they are still joined one to the other, and are still able to be circular. When once, however, the wedge-shaped characters, losing more and more of their original hieroglyphic form, had come into vogue, the superior quickness and ease with which they could be written soon made them universally prevalent. The literary activity, of which Chaldea was now the centre, made rapid writing of great importance, and so this cursive hand, as we may term the cuneiform, came to be exclusively used. Further simplication was of course only a matter of time.

Now a hieroglyphic system of writing has to represent ideas as well as objects, and just as language expresses the spiritual through the veil of material metaphor, so hieroglyphic writing must symbolise ideas by means of objects. Thus *two legs* may denote "walking," *a hand* may denote "to seize," *breath* may denote "the soul." But it is plain that the same object may represent more than one conception; *two legs* may stand for "going," "running," "standing," "support," and even "growth," as well as for "walking." Every hieroglyphic, therefore, may be pronounced in a variety of different ways, according to its significations; and since few languages are so poor as to be without synonymes, it may be pronounced in more than one way, even when the same thing is meant. This will certainly be the case where the same hieroglyphic system of writing is used by tribes who speak different dialects; the Chinese, for instance, have one set of written characters, but the variety of idioms spoken in the empire cause the same character to be sounded in one way at Canton, and in another at Pekin. So long as the writing continues to be purely hieroglyphic, all this produces no confusion; on the contrary it facilitates intercourse and civilisation. But wherever there is any pretence to progressive culture, no writing *can* long continue purely hieroglyphic; although the native proper names may all be significant, and so reducible to hieroglyphic representation, it is quite otherwise with foreign proper names, and, however much a people may wish to confine themselves within their own boundaries, like the Egyptians of the Old Empire, or the Chinese of to-day, they will find themselves brought into contact with unallied nations, and compelled to chronicle their foreign as well as their home policy.[1] Sooner or later these troublesome proper names will have to be written *phonetically*, that is, in hieroglyphics which are void of meaning, and so have ceased to be hieroglyphics, but are sounded in some

[1] As in Egypt, the oldest names given by the early Accadian inhabitants of Babylonia to their neighbours were of native origin like *numma*, Elam, "high;" *Śubarti*, Syria, of the same signification, and not the names by which those neighbours called themselves.

particular way. Out of the different pronunciations which can be attached to a certain character, it will be necessary to select some which it shall represent when used simply as the symbol of a particular phonetic power. The obvious course, under these circumstances, might have seemed to select a single phonetic power and attach it invariably to a character when non-significant; but obvious as such a procedure appears to us, it was not so obvious to the old inventors of writing, and in numberless instances they allowed a character to carry more than one value. What value, however, was meant in any particular case was pointed out in several ways. In certain combinations, a polyphone had always to be read with one special value and no other, or the pronunciation attached to some object or idea which seemed suitable to the individual or country denoted was chosen, or again, the pronunciation was determined by the vowel of the character pre-ceding or following, supposing that the syllable was an open one. Thus we know that the second character in the name of *Gungunuv* must be sounded *un*, because the vowel of the first syllable is *u*; and we might have concluded, without the additional help of a gloss, that the second character (⭲⭰) in the name of *Ansan* or south-western Elam was to be pronounced *sa*, and not *du*, on account of the last syllable beginning with *a*.[1]

Of course the application of the merely phonetic employment of the old hieroglyphics would be extended as soon as its convenience had been found out. One of the first uses to which it would be put would be to express the pronouns, which must have been a sore puzzle as long as there was only a picture-writing to draw upon. In the Semitic and Aryan families, indeed, the whole grammatical machinery of the language, the nerves and blood-vessels that give life to the bare skeleton, would have been an equal puzzle. Even the prepositions would have wanted some other mode of representation than that of hieroglyphic writing. But the inventors of the cuneiform were neither Semites nor Aryans, nor did they speak an inflectional language of any kind. I should not, indeed, like to go so far as to say that the invention of a purely hieroglyphical system of writing is inconceivable among those who speak what are called inflectional languages, more especially as the Hamath legends seem to show that an independent hieroglyphic system of home

---

[1] Since the character in question had the signification of "going" when used as an ideograph, it would seem that *sa* meant "to go" in the language of Susa.

growth was in use among the inhabitants of northern Syria, while the grammar at least of Old Egyptian has striking affinities to the Semitic ; but it is difficult to understand how such a system of writing could have originated except among those in whose idioms every grammatical suffix was a word of full and independent meaning, and where the same root or vocable was equally a noun, a verb, or an adverb. Whatever may be said about its grammar, the lexicon at least of Old Egyptian fully answers to these requirements ; and the grammatical character of Chinese and Mexican is well known, while it may yet turn out that the hieroglyphics of Hamath were borrowed by the Semitic population from a non-Semitic people, such as I believe the Hittites to have been. *Primâ facie* evidence is certainly against the assumption that either Semite or Aryan could ever have invented a system of ideographs.

The inventors of the *cuneiform* system of writing, at all events, spoke an agglutinative language. This is one of the most interesting and important results obtained from the decipherment of the inscriptions, and explains at once the difficulties and peculiarities which a first view of the Assyrian syllabary presents. The Assyrians called the agglutinative idiom of their predecessors Accadian, in distinction from their own Semitic speech ;[1] and a certain knowledge of Accadian is essential for a right understanding of the mode of writing which we are engaged upon. Thus the ideograph which means " a corpse " ▶◀ also signifies " to open," two ideas which have nothing

---

[1] This seems to me (as to Lenormant, Schrader, and Delitzsch) to result from the correct translation of a colophon attached to a bilingual (Accadian and Assyrian) vocabulary in *W. A. I.* II., 36, 1 *Rev.*, lines 10 *sq.*, where we read : " According to the old tablets and papyri (*literally*, vegetable of knowledge), the parallel writings of Assyria and Accad." In *W. A. I.* III., 55, 2, 9 *sq.* we have " (The appearances) of the star Curuna (of the Vine) : (compiled for Esar-haddon) king of multitudes, king of Assyria, son of Sennacherib, king of multitudes, king of the same Assyria (according to the tablets and papyri), the parallel writings of Assyria, of Sumir, and of Accad." Here the original Accadian text is not given. In *W. A. I.* III., 64 *Rev.*, 32, we find " according to the papyri of the tablet, the parallel writings of Babylon." These passages show either that Accad is opposed to Assyria and Sumir which is placed next to Assyria, or that Assyria is opposed to both Sumir and Accad. In any case, the first passage contrasts Assyria and Accad ; the last passage proves that translations from Accadian were made for the ancient library of Babylon after the latter city had passed into the possession of the Semitic race. As to the question whether Sumir denoted the " Turanian " or the Semitic population of Chaldea, my belief is that it originally signified the lowland " Turanian " population of the country which the Accadians found there on their descent from the mountains of Elam ; as this was the first part of Babylonia to be occupied by the Semitic conquerors, however, the word Sumir afterwards came to designate the Semitic Babylonians.

in common; and the ideograph which stands for "fortress" is also used in the sense of "death." But the whole mystery is cleared up as soon as we know that *bat* in Accadian meant "to open," and "a fortress," as well as "a corpse" or "death;" and the fact that the same character is employed indifferently for "corpse" and "open," only shows that the Accadians had elaborated their method of writing sufficiently to apply the symbol of some idea to the expression of some other idea which was called by the same name. But the reason of anything apparently so arbitrary would have been sought in vain without the key furnished by the old Accadian language.

As we shall see hereafter, the Semites, first in north-western Babylonia, and afterwards throughout the valleys of the Euphrates and Tigris, took possession of the country and cities of the Accadians, and gradually extirpated their language, appropriating their arts and sciences, and above all, their system of writing. This was developed and improved, just as the Phœnicians, though not originating the art of writing, took the hieroglyphics of Egypt, and out of that cumbrous machinery perfected the Kadmeian alphabet. The Eastern Semite, whose initiation into culture was earlier than that of his western brother, did not arrive at anything so perfect, greatly as he improved upon the heritage left him by an alien race: the result of his labours was the Assyrian syllabary. The principle adopted in the formation of it was this. The Accadian values of the characters which were significant words in the old language, were employed as mere phonetic sounds: *me*, for instance, the pronunciation of , no longer represented "a gathering," but simply an unmeaning syllable. The way, no doubt, had already been prepared by the Accadians in the case of proper names and a few other words; but the extension and consistent carrying out of the principle was reserved for the Semitic Assyrians. Why they should have kept all, or at least many, of the numerous values which a single ideograph was able to bear, is far from clear: it added immensely to the complexity of their writing, and the contrivances by which the confusion arising from it was sought to be avoided will be discussed in the next lecture. The most probable explanation is that this remodelling of the writing was both gradual, and the work of persons who spoke Accadian as well as Assyrian. Very often the scribes would still be Accadians; and to one who was acquainted with the Accadian language, a particular character, even though ordinarily standing for another phonetic value, might more readily occur as the representative of a certain sound than a different ideograph which had been already set apart for the purpose. Thus a scribe who wanted to express the syllable *dan* or *lib* might think of ⊢⫪⫪ before any other character, and use it accordingly, although it had already been determined that ⊢⫪⫪ should represent *cal* in the new syllabary. We must not forget that the Accadians had themselves begun to use their ideographs as phonetic characters, so that several of them would be already polyphonous, and the example thus set, especially if the scribes were Accadians, or were brought up under Accadian instruction (as we know must have been the case), would inevitably be followed. To the same cause must be ascribed the retention of the use of the characters as ideographs. It was found convenient to retain certain of them as determinative prefixes, one (⫪) to mark an individual, another (⫯⫯) to mark a country, and so on, while brevity and rapidity were aided by an ideographic writing. Hence the hieroglyphic origin of the characters was never forgotten; and up to the latest days of the Assyrian monarchy every character could be used as an ideograph as well as to denote a phonetic sound. Of course, these ideographs, when they occur in an Assyrian inscription, have to be read as Assyrian words : ⊢ , for example, will not be *me*, but some grammatical form of the root קלה "to assemble," or *ramcu*, "a herd." We may lay it down as a general rule that the Assyrian translation of the meaning of an ideograph was never used as a phonetic value; that office was left for the Accadian words to fill. It often enough happens that the phonetic value is met with under a slightly changed form as the Assyrian rendering of the ideograph; but this is only because the Turanian word has been borrowed by the Assyrians and subjected to such modifications as were needed to make it conform to the structure and grammar of the Semitic tongues. Thus, ⊢⊤ *muk*, "a building," becomes *muccu*; ⫪⊢☐ *nanga*, "a town," becomes *nagu;* ⊢⊤ ⊢⫪⫪ *lamma*, "colossus," *lamassu*, etc. I hope to show hereafter how numerous these loan words are, and what an important testimony they bear, not only to the debt of the Semite to the Turanian in the matter of civilization, but also to the primitive triliteralism of Semitic speech. The general rule, however, which I have just been stating, admits of one or two exceptions. The sound *iz* (*its*, *is̆*) was com-

3*

monly denoted by ⊒, a character which signifies "tree," and is used as a
determinative prefix whenever trees are spoken of. But the Accadian word
for "tree" was *gis*, a value which ⊒ frequently has, *iz* or rather *ets* (ץצ)
being of Semitic derivation and not employed by the Accadians as a phonetic
power of this character. It is possible, however, that *ets* (*iz*) is really borrowed
from the Accadian *gis* (Semitic צ generally answering to Accadian *g*); and in
any case its use as a determinative prefix, when it was not pronounced in
reading, had much to do with its pronunciation coming to be regarded as
purely phonetic and non-significant. Nearly all other *certain* instances of the
Assyrian origin of phonetic powers are to be found in the case of determinatives.

I have noticed above how inevitably a number of different pronunciations
or sounds will attach themselves to an ideograph. All the causes which
bring about their multiplication were at work among the Accadians. Here
was a people well advanced in culture, and whose language, therefore, would
be correspondingly rich, and abound in synonymes. They had, moreover,
elaborated their system of writing, and endeavoured by various contrivances
to make the smallest number of symbols express the largest number of ideas,
as the case of the ideograph for " corpse " and " open " will show; while
dialects in plenty flourished in Chaldea. Berosus says that " a great number
of heterogeneous tribes inhabited Khaldea,"[1] and at least two Turanian idioms
may be detected in the bilingual tablets. The first idea of writing and the
first hieroglyphics originated among the mountains of Elam before the
Accadai or " Highlanders " had descended into the alluvial plains below, and
Elam up to a late period abounded in dialects. The polyphonous character
of the Assyrian syllabary, therefore, is by no means surprising; our only
wonder is that it is not greater. As it is, however, the task of learning the
whole of it proved too severe for the ordinary man, and when Assur-bani-pal
wished to give some sort of education to the mass of the people, and enable
the foreigners at his court to read a writing the knowledge of which had
hitherto been confined to the privileged few, he was obliged to have syllabaria
compiled which have done more to give us an insight into the nature of
Assyrian writing than years of patient labour could have done. The king
tell us that " Nebo and Tasmit had made large his ears, and given sight to
his eyes," so that he caused the old learning of Accad, and the syllabaria that

[1] *Apud Syncelli Chronicon*, p. 28.

explain it, to be written down and stored "in the midst of the palace for the inspection of" his "people;" and the final words, "of my people," are very noticeable. Trade in Western Asia had long been in a most flourishing condition; the merchants of the east and the west met at Carchemish and Nineveh; houses were sold and let and money lent at interest, while numberless contract-tablets and other private documents attest that the necessities of commerce had obliged a considerable part of the population to acquaint themselves at any rate with "the three R's." Now Aramaic had become the common language of trade as of diplomacy, and the convenient Phœnician alphabet was already threatening to supplant the syllabary of Assyria. To prevent such a humiliation, such a visible symbol that the sceptre was passing from Assyria to Palestine, it was needful to popularise the Assyrian system of writing; and this necessity, as the inscriptions just quoted inform us, was far more potent than the requirements of the foreigners from Greece and Lydia, from Egypt and Cyprus, from Arabia and even India, or than the spirit of an age which resembled that of the Alexandrine grammarians. The syllabaria, which were drawn up by order of the king, usually consist of three columns: in the middle is the character to be explained, while the left hand column gives its phonetic powers, and the right hand column the Assyrian translation of each of these powers when regarded as Accadian words. In the right hand column, consequently, the characters are treated as ideographs, in the left hand column as phonetic symbols so far as Assyrian is concerned. The careful rendering of each of the Accadian words (*i.e.* of Assyrian phonetic powers) is due to the interest felt at this time in the study of the long-dead language of Chaldea, and to which we owe the preservation and translation of numberless specimens of Accadian literature.

A syllabary discovered by Mr. Smith when excavating at Kouyundjik on behalf of the *Daily Telegraph*, contains a fourth column giving the Assyrian synonymes of the word by which the ideograph is rendered.[1] This is not the first instance of a table of Semitic synonymes; long lists of these, with or without Accadian equivalents, and forming a dictionary in the true sense of the word, are among the treasures of the British Museum, while

---

[1] The syllabary is published in the IVth volume of the *Cuneiform Inscriptions of Western Asia*, plates 69, 70. In the majority of instances the word given in the third column is an Assyrianised form of the Accadian word in the first column.

other tablets, after setting down a literal translation of the Accadian names of birds, plants, stones, etc., append the ordinary Assyrian terms in a third column.

With this transition of the syllabary into a dictionary I must conclude the present lecture. It is not too much to say that the first native lexicon, the first forerunner of the works of Johnson and of Grimm, arose out of the complex peculiarities of the Assyrian method of writing. In my next lecture I shall have to consider the defects of this method, and the devices whereby the Assyrians in transcribing, and we in deciphering, have endeavoured to meet and overcome them. This will lead us on to a review of the various modifications undergone by the syllabary when adopted by foreign neighbours, until it was finally simplified into an alphabet under the influence of the practical Aryan mind.

LECTURE III.

The Syllabary, continued.

—•—

YOU will remember my remarking in the last lecture that the Accadian inventors of the cuneiform system of writing gave proof of their progress in culture by their attempt to express the largest number of ideas by the smallest number of symbols. One of the most obvious ways of effecting this would be by the combination of ideographs; thus "papyrus" might be represented by the hieroglyphics of "writing" and "water," preceded by the determinative of "vegetable," ⊨|║| and "the act of drinking" by putting the symbol of "water" inside the symbol of "mouth," ⊨⧈. Such a proceeding would be suggested and assisted by the agglutinative character of the language itself, in which the derivatives of inflectional idioms were replaced by compounds, each member of the compound retaining its full independent meaning and tone. Thus the idea of "king" was expressed by the compound *un-gal* "great man," and when it was wanted to represent this idea in writing nothing was easier than to combine the ideographs of "man" and "great," Hieratic ⊟║⊏ whence the Archaic ⊟⧉ and Assyrian ⊨⧉. The plan once adopted was carried out very extensively, and one of our chief difficulties in the reconstruction of the ancient Accadian speech is to know when a compound really existed in the spoken language, or when it did so in the writing alone. We happen to know that the group of characters ⊨|║| ⁂ ⊷ which literally signify "house of the land of the corpse," reading *ê-mad-bat*, must be pronounced *arali*, and denote "death" or "Hades;" we also happen to know that the particle "thus," or "if," which is written in characters which respectively read *su-gar-tur-lal* 𒄀 𒌋 𒌓 𒆷 was sounded *sugarturlal* as well as *tucundi;*[1] but numberless cases occur in which our present state of knowledge does not allow us to determine whether the combination existed for the ear as well as for the eye. Considering the nature of the language, it is necessary, when any doubt exists, to assume that the compound ideograph really represents a spoken compound, until the assumption is disproved. The Assyrian scribes generally regarded these compound ideographs as actual words, giving a literal translation of them in one column, and the Semitic name of the object signified in another. For purely Assyrian purposes, however, it did not matter whether an ideograph were compound or simple; in either case the notion it conveyed had to be expressed by a word which did not bear the slightest relation to the character written down. The most cumbrous compound ideographs, however, were dropped by the Assyrians; beyond this the Accadian system was adopted bodily, though with the important difference that whereas in Accadian these compound ideographs had been phonetic as well as significant, in Assyrian they became mere signs. Here, then, is one of the defects connected with the cuneiform method of writing when applied to the expression of Assyrian. We have no clue to the *Assyrian* pronunciation of a character when used as an ideograph, unless that pronunciation be given us by the Assyrians themselves; and our knowledge of the meaning of each member of a group of ideographs, and, therefore, of the whole group itself, will not aid us in the slightest towards discovering the Assyrian pronunciation of the group, although we may be thoroughly acquainted with the pronunciation of each separate ideograph. In Accadian, finding that *un* "man," and *gal* "great," when combined together meant "king," we may conclude that "a king" was called *ungal;* but unless we knew from other sources that "a king" was termed *sarru* in Assyrian, our knowledge that *nisu* was "man," and *rabu* "great" in that language, would not help us towards the discovery of the fact. The retention of compound ideographs, therefore, increases the difficulties and labour of the decipherer of Semitic Assyrian; and as this is a difficulty which naturally would not have been felt by the Assyrians themselves, we can only get over it by the patient comparison of variant readings which may substitute in one text the phonetic reading of an ideograph which

---

[1] I accept this on M. Lenormant's authority, but I confess to feeling very doubtful myself whether the four characters in question were ever pronounced otherwise than as *tucundi*. The final syllable of the latter word is the affix *da* which becomes *di* after *u*, as in *Dungi* "the mighty one" for *Dun-ga*.

occurs in another, or by the assiduous examination of the bilingual tablets. Indeed, without the latter, our knowledge of Assyrian on this side at least must always have remained extremely imperfect.

But the difficulties presented by the compound ideographs are only an intensification of those presented by the simple ones. The same idea might have been denoted by several different words; and the syllabary of four columns referred to in the last lecture shows to how great an extent this was actually the case. The translator accordingly is continually being confronted by the question what Assyrian root out of many possible ones he is to assign to an ideograph in a particular passage. This difficulty is chiefly met with in the case of proper names, which are so often written ideographically; and one of the main causes of distrust with which the interpretation of the Assyrian inscriptions was at first received was due to the uncertainty attached to the reading of the proper names. Outsiders could not understand how any confidence could be placed in the renderings of these mysterious legends when the translators differed so materially from one another, and from themselves at different times, in their transliteration of royal names, a problem that seemed so much simpler than that of translation, and, indeed, a necessary preliminary of it. Had it not been for a variant reading which gave the true phonetic representation, we should never have known that the second element in the name of Rimmon-nirari, which had been variously read *venkh*, *zallus*, and *likhkhus* ⟨glyph⟩, was really pronounced *nirari*, "my help," by the Assyrians; and even now, the name of the Air-god, whom I have called Rimmon on the authority of certain glosses in the bilingual tablets, is given as Vul, Ao, and Bin by other scholars.[1] Perhaps the most provoking case of uncertainty in which this use of ideographs by the Assyrians has left us is that of the chief personages in the great Babylonian epic, of which the story of the deluge forms the eleventh

---

[1] My reading of the name as Rimmon is based upon several reasons. (1) A mythological tablet expressly interprets the name of the god by *Rammânu*. (2) The original meaning of the name of the god, ⟨glyph⟩, is "wind" or "breath;" from which came the signification of "self," *ramanu* in Assyrian. Hence in the bilingual tablets ⟨glyph⟩ *im* is generally rendered *ramanu*. (3) Dr. Schrader has pointed out that the name of the god is written *Ra-man* and (*Ra-*)*ma-nu* in the name of an eponyme (Canons I., II., *IV. A. I.* II., 68, 2, 21). He has also noticed that the name of another eponyme, *Bar-ku-lid-an-ni* (*IV. A. I.* III., 47, 3, 8, compared with *IV. A. I.* III., 2, 20; II., 68, 2, 2, 29), proves that the god was sometimes called *Barku* "the Lightning" in Assyrian.

lay. The name of the solar hero around whom the whole epic centres is written with three characters ⟨cuneiform⟩ which phonetically would be sounded *Gis*, *dhu*, and *bar* or *mas*. The first character would be *gis*, and not *iz*, as Mr. Smith reads, since *iz* was an Assyrian and not an Accadian value. The name was certainly not pronounced *Gisdhubar* by the Assyrians; and it is more than doubtful whether it was so even by the Accadians, as the word seems to mean " body " or " mass of fire," from *dhu*, ⟨cuneiform⟩ " mass," and a compound ideograph which literally signifies " wood bound " or " bundle of faggots," and was used to denote " fire," ⟨cuneiform⟩. The latter idea was expressed in Accadian by several different words, and we are no more warranted in thinking that " fire " was ever called *gisbar*, than we are in thinking that the two characters ⟨cuneiform⟩, literally " wood-holding," which are employed as a synonyme of " king " in allusion to the wooden sceptre he wielded and used in this sense as a title of Gisdhubar[1] himself, were ever sounded *gis-tuk*. The name of the Chaldean Noah has been equally a matter of dispute. Mr. Smith originally conjectured *Sisit* in reference to the Sisuthrus of Berosus; but Sisuthrus apparently turns out to be Khasis-adra.[2] Now the Accadian name that appears in the Erech version of the account of the Deluge which we possess, means " the Sun of life;" and since *zi* was " life " in Accadian, and *tam* one of the terms by which the sun was known, the whole word might easily be read Tam-zi. There are several reasons which lead to the identification of Tam-zi with the well-known Tammuz; among others, the fact that the month Tammuz was called Dūzu by the Assyrians, Du-zi " the son of life " being husband of Istar and a form of Tam-zi;[3] and it seems to me, therefore, that we are thus enabled to arrive at the true Accadian pronunciation of the name. But the very uncertainty in which it is involved is a good illustration of the obstacle afforded by ideographic writing to the progress of Assyrian decipherment. It is this which makes the reading of the astrological tablets so peculiarly difficult. They were composed at a time when the Semitic settlers in Babylonia were beginning to learn the arts and sciences of their Accadian neighbours; the resolution of the writing of the latter into a series of mere phonetic signs had not yet been completed, and the ideographs in which the Accadians had

[1] See Note 1 in the Appendix at the end of the chapter.
[2] See Note 2 in the Appendix.   [3] See Note 3 in the Appendix.

made their astrological memoranda were reproduced in full, eked out here and there by Semitic words and grammatical suffixes. Even the technical terms which the original inhabitants of Chaldea had written out phonetically were allowed to remain, though the pronunciation of the corresponding Assyrian word was attached to them: thus *ri-ba-an-na*, "conjunction" was still written, though it was now sounded *kas-ri-tu* (literally "bond"). The fact that the same character might stand for several wholly different ideas adds greatly to the difficulty of these astrological documents; and no attempts were made to lessen these difficulties, as in the case of other inscriptions, since it was wished to confine sacred knowledge of all kinds to as narrow a circle as possible. Hence these astrological tablets can only be puzzled out by means of a tolerably wide comparison of passages and a minute investigation of the bilingual tablets; and the endeavour I have made[1] to give literal translations of the astrological documents, published in the third volume of *Western Asiatic Inscriptions*, will, I hope, form a basis for further work in this interesting direction. When the particular ideographic force of a character in these tablets has once been determined, the use of picture-signs renders translation easier than it would be had we to deal with spelt-out words of uncertain derivation or uncertain application: thus we know that ▷◁⊞, in which the ideograph of "black" is placed inside the ideograph of "face" must mean "black face" or "shadow," and ╡╡╪ ⧻, "horned," tells us its signification with greater certainty than does its Semitic equivalent *karunu*.

This leads me to speak of the advantages resulting from the use of ideographs which counterbalance its inconveniences. We often find some Assyrian root of unknown signification interchanging with an ideograph with the meaning of which we are already acquainted; and, should the context suit, we are thus enabled to fix the sense of a new word. It is the compound ideograph, however, in which the superior advantage of picture over phonetic writing to the decipherer comes most prominently into view. A large proportion of the ideographs are compound, and it naturally happens that the ideas represented by compound ideographs are less likely to be denoted by Assyrian words the forms or special senses of which are readily to be detected in the cognate idioms; hence we can not unfrequently

[1] In the *Transactions of the Society of Biblical Archæology*, Vol. III., p. 1.

determine the sense of an obscure Semitic root by observing the nature of the compound ideograph to which it answers.

But even as regards simple ideographs the Assyrians were not without means of evading the drawbacks occasioned by the fact that the same character might be pronounced in more than one fashion. Except in the case of astrology and kindred subjects, the object of an inscription was to be read with the greatest ease possible. The employment of ideographs was serviceable to the writer; but the reader equally demanded that this should cause him no additional trouble. An inscription was not a puzzle for the exercise of ingenuity; and pains had to be taken that mistakes should not be made in reading it, or time wasted in making it out. So far as the difficulty of choosing one out of several possible pronunciations of an ideograph was concerned, the Assyrians felt it as much as we do; and accordingly, except where they had to do with very familiar terms, they betook themselves to the contrivance of phonetic complements which gave the first or last letters of the word they intended to be read in each particular instance. These phonetic complements may be divided into two groups, grammatical and lexical. An ideograph lacked all marks of grammatical relation; it might be a noun or an adverb, or a verb of any tense, mood, or person; where, therefore, the context did not show clearly beyond the possibility of error to what part of speech it belonged, a character was either prefixed or affixed, or both, to indicate how the word was to be read. Thus ⸰⸰ *ACS-ud* "I conquered," but ⸰⸰ *CISID-ti* "acquisition." Generally, when the grammatical indices were affixed, the syllabic nature of the writing allowed the grammatical relation to be pointed out as well as the root; thus ⸰⸰ may be represented in Assyrian by *nadanu* "to give," *sumu* "name," and *santu* "year;" but when we meet with ⸰⸰ ⸰⸰ we must read *IDD-in* "he gave" (root נתן=נדן), when ⸰⸰ *S-um* "name," when ⸰⸰ ⸰⸰ *S-an-na* "year," and so on. It is sometimes difficult, though very rarely so except in the astrological tablets, to decide whether two or more characters are to be considered an ideograph with its phonetic complement, or a phonetically spelled-out word; only the context, for example, can tell us whether ⸰⸰ is *mu-tuv* "death," or *SANA-tuv* "year." The uncertainty here is parallel to the doubt which arises when a compound ideograph happens to have exactly the same form as an Assyrian word; Is ⸰⸰, we may ask, an

Accadian term, *i.e.*, a compound ideograph, or is it the oblique case of *khisu* "a crown?" Of course a doubt of this sort can only arise when the compound ideograph is not amalgamated into one character, but expressed by a series of characters separated one from the other. Such doubts can only be settled by a comparison of passages and a practical familiarity with the inscriptions.

There are certain cases, of no great frequency however, which have to be carefully distinguished from the use of ideographs. We sometimes come across abbreviations of common Assyrian words which differ from ideographs just as in English symbols like *viz.* or *i.e.* differ from abbreviations like *wh.* or *shd.* Such abbreviated words, however, in the inscriptions are very few, and they are usually found at the end of lines. *Ci* sometimes stands for *cinu*, *cinatu* "firm," *mu* for *musu* "night," *cis* for *cissu*, *cissatu* "many," *li* for *livitu* "bordering on." I hardly think that the abbreviated forms of the prepositions *ci* for *civa*, *it* for *itti*, etc., belong here: when we look at the cognate dialects it seems necessary to conclude that the shortened forms were used in speaking as well as in writing. Such abbreviated forms were never employed by the scribe except where there was no risk of error on the part of the reader, and accordingly they are not one of the difficulties experienced by the modern decipherer.

I have thus far dwelt upon the difficulties we experience from the use of simple ideographs: I must now turn to the other side of the picture and point out that these difficulties are counterbalanced by corresponding advantages. In the first place, under the form of determinative prefixes, they serve to divide words and to mark the existence and character of proper names in a sentence. The upright wedge ⟨wedge⟩ denotes that the name of an individual follows, and the names of women, countries, cities, vegetable substances, stones, grasses, birds, and animals are respectively preceded by the determinative ideographs, a list of which will be found in my *Elementary Assyrian Grammar*. The ideograph of the plural ⟨cuneiform⟩, which may be termed a determinative affix, is equally useful in showing the number of a noun as well as in marking its end. This plural affix is often added to the phonetically expressed plural ending; thus we may have ⟨cuneiform⟩ *sarr-a-ni* "kings," besides ⟨cuneiform⟩ and ⟨cuneiform⟩. The determinative prefixes were, of course, not usually pronounced; they appealed to the eye alone, not to the ear. The exception to this rule would take place only when the gentilic adjective was written after the ideograph of "country" or "city," instead of the local name; ⊀ 𒈨𒌷𒅆𒄯𒀀, for instance, must be read *mat Yahudai* "land of the Jews." The second advantage which we derive from the employment of ideographs has already been noticed; it is the clue given to the signification of an Assyrian word, otherwise unknown, by its being interchanged with an ideograph of familiar meaning. It is an advantage which this mode of writing in Assyrian shares with all others of pictorial origin.

To pass now from the ideographic to the phonetic use of the Assyrian characters. Here we are met by the existence of polyphones, that great standing difficulty in the way of decipherment, and the chief cause of the scepticism with which it was at first received. In the last lecture I have traced the origin of it, and shown how what seemed an insuperable objection to the correctness of the key applied to the interpretation of the inscriptions has turned out to be one of its surest proofs. The variant values which it was demonstrated the same sign must possess if the system of decipherment were correct are actually assigned to the sign in the so-called *syllabaria*, and what we now know to have been the origin and primary nature of the whole cuneiform writing necessitates their existence. But the practical difficulties caused by their existence remain, and, speaking roughly, can only be got over by experience. Certain general rules, however, may be laid down for determining what particular power shall be assigned to a character in a given instance. These rules, it is true, are not universally valid, and cases will even arise in which the most practised experience will be at fault. But such cases are rare, and are getting rarer every day: indeed, we may say that they are almost entirely confined to proper names and to words of infrequent occurrence, of which there are no variant readings, or else to those which may be derived from two different roots of similar signification. Before laying down the rules, however, it is as well to observe that the student need not trouble himself about the existence of homophones. Homophones are rare, the Assyrians having usually dropped a phonetic power belonging to one character which happened to be the same as one possessed by another. A reference to the syllabary will show how scanty such cases are, whether the syllables are open (that is, beginning or ending with a vowel) or closed (that is, with a vowel between two consonants). It is perhaps noticeable that the three chief vowels, *a*, *i*, and *u*, may all be represented by two characters, ⫯⫯ and ⊨⊢ for *a*, ⊨⊨ and 𝍈 for *i*, and ⊨⫯⫯⫯⊨ and ◀ for *u*; but it is probable that when the second of either of these characters was used, it was intended to mark the absence of an initial breathing. This at all events was true of ⊨⫯⫯⫯⊨ and ◀. It must be remembered that the Assyrians were not composing enigmas; they wished their inscriptions to be read; and accordingly everything was done to facilitate the reading of them and to remove the difficulties inherent in a polyphonic system of writing. The chief rules, then, observed by the scribes (and, therefore, also by the readers) in the choice of one out of many possible values assignable to a character are these :—

(1) The existence of an ideograph should never be arbitrarily assumed unless the inscription (like the astrological ones generally) is written throughout ideographically rather than phonetically. If phonetic complements or other indications of the presence of an ideograph are wanting, every resource should be tried before taking the character in an ideographic sense. It was the neglect of this rule which enabled M. Oppert to get *saldha ebus* and *tsiba ieris* out of *saldhac* and *tsiba'aca*, and thus to overlook two important instances of a remarkable grammatical form.

(2) The triliteral character of the Assyrian language is a sure and constant guide in the selection of our readings. Quadriliteral roots, mostly formed by the insertion of *r* or *l*, are few in number, and an acquaintance with them can soon be acquired. When, therefore, we find that only one value of a particular character will allow of a triliteral root, all other values leading to quadriliteral or even quinqueliteral ones, we may feel no hesitation as to the reading to be adopted. Thus when we come across a word like ⫸⫯⫯⫯⫯ we know that the only one of the many values of the middle character that will give a triliteral word is *dan* (*mu-dan-nin*).

(3) The scribes generally gave a clue to the reading by doubling the consonant, that is, by terminating the preceding syllable or beginning the following syllable with the initial or final letter of the sound which they desired should be given to the character used. Not only a *dageshed* letter but a long or accented syllable also was marked by the repetition of the following consonant; and the frequent occurrence, therefore, of these double consonants is one of our principal helps in determining the reading of a word. Thus

we know that 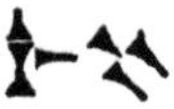 must be read *sal-lat* "spoil,"  *ag-gul-lu* "wheel," and so on.

(4) A knowledge of the grammar and lexicon, as well as of the structure of the language is indispensable towards settling the reading of a word. Just as philological reasons must supply the vowels in Hebrew and Phœnician or the double letters in Æthiopic, so they have often to fix the pronunciation of a character in Assyrian. The grammatical laws of the language alone will frequently determine whether a terminal  is to be read as *ut* or *tav* or *tu*, whether  is to be *nuv* or *niv*, whether  is *mur*, *cin*, or *khar*. But the lexicon also performs the same function. It is seldom that we have a doubtful case like  "an oracle," where the second character may be read either *ris* or *sak*, and derived with an equal show of reason from פרש or فسق; the existence of a particular root in Assyrian itself or the cognate dialects generally settles the question of reading without further trouble. Thus the existence of the root מכר "to sell," not only in the other Semitic idioms, but also in Assyrian, shows us clearly how  *nam-cur*, "saleable thing," or "goods," is to be transliterated, even apart from the fact that we once find a final *ri* which obliges us to select *cur* out of the numerous values of , on pain of breaking our second rule.[1]

(5) Variant readings of the same passage are a great assistance, more especially in the case of initial characters. Under the head of variant readings, we may include variant forms of the same word, one form often determining the special letter or letters belonging to the root. Thus  has been read *khatstsi* and compared with the root חזה "to see;" but the variant  *tir-tsi* shows that the word is *tar-tsi* (comp. ترص).

(6) Speaking generally, an open syllable is to be preferred to a closed one when a character has both powers. *Ri*, for instance, is to be preferred to *tal* when we meet with . Usually, whenever a character which was ordinarily employed as an open syllable was to be read as a closed one, the fact was pointed out in the way mentioned under the head of the third rule.

(7) Common use had set apart one or two special values for each character, and unless the action of the other rules interfere, these common

[1] It was the neglect of this rule that caused Mr. Norris in his *Assyrian Dictionary* to read the word in question as "*nimmat*," which he had considerable difficulty in connecting with "*nimmatri*." The character which he reads *nim* should be *nam*.

and favourite values ought to be read in a doubtful instance. Practical experience of course can alone decide what these common and favourite values are; but a slight acquaintance with the inscriptions will enable us to determine them in the larger number of cases. Thus *tar* and *cut* are more usual powers of ▶◣ than *khaz* or *sil*, ◄ is more frequently *bat* than *til*, and ⊨⫼ more often stands for *dan* or *cal* than for *lab* or *rib*.

(8) The 8th rule is that a character which represents a syllable beginning with a vowel is very rarely used after one which terminates in a consonant, and if an apparent case of this kind occur, the presumption is that the first character is to be read as an ideograph, the second being its phonetic complement. Thus ▶⫼◀�⊨⫼ is to be read *ri-e'-uv* "shepherd," and not *ri-bit-uv*. This rule, however, admits of exceptions.

(9) The 9th and last rule is one that has been of great assistance in deciphering inscriptions which like those of Assyria do not divide the words from one another. A word always ends with a line, and a line ends with a word. Three or four exceptions, at most, can be found to this rule, and even these occur in the case of proper names like Shalman-eser in a brick legend lately brought home by Mr. George Smith.[1]

These, then, are the nine practical rules by which the student may be guided in his transliteration of the inscriptions. They materially lessen the difficulties resulting from the use of polyphones, even though they cannot be said to remove them altogether. But there is a drawback inherent in the Assyrian syllabary, and quite apart from the polyphony of the characters, which I have not yet touched upon, although it is really the most serious defect in the cuneiform system of writing. This system, we have seen, was originally intended to express the sounds and ideas of a Turanian language, and its application to a Semitic speech was a later adaptation. Now we all know how impossible it is to express the phonology of one language in the alphabet of another. Sounds which are wanting in the one may be fully developed in the other, while the needs of the scribe may confuse several distinct letters under one and the same character. All this and more has happened in the case of the Assyrian syllabary. Accadian was poor in

[1] It is hardly necessary to observe that when two characters (such as *ca* and *ac*) come together, the first of which ends with the same vowel as that with which the second begins, we may infer that they form one closed syllable (as *cac*).

sibilants and dentals. So ⊬⊬ has to do duty for *za* (זַא), and *tsa* (צַא), and ⊨⊬⊬ for *da* (דָא), and *dha* (טָא). The vocalic ⊨⊬⊬ was taken to represent the peculiarly Semitic *ayin*, and different shades of sound are accordingly confused together in it. But the mischief was least apparent in open syllables, at least in those which terminated in a vowel. It was in closed syllables, and in those which ended with a consonant, that the confusion was greatest. The Accadian made no distinction between the different dentals and labials at the end of a syllable; the Semite accordingly who borrowed his writing had to represent *ad*, *adh* and *at*, *ab* and *ap* by one and the same character. The Accadian blurred the sibilants; the Assyrian, therefore, had to use 𒉽 for *sir*, *zir*, *śir*, and *tsir*. The Accadian *m* was really *mv*; the Assyrian consequently was forced to use the same character for both *m* and *v*. The Accadian was unacquainted with the sound *yu*, and so the Assyrian had to write the first and third persons of certain conjugations with the same character (𒀀), though in the one case it was to be read *'u* (אוּ), and in the other *yu* (יִי). The consequent uncertainty as to the terminal or initial consonant of a syllable would naturally not press upon the Assyrian, who would instinctively know what words were required by his language in a given instance; but it *does* press seriously upon us who are often at a loss as to the root to which we must assign a particular word. Does the first syllable of ◄𒌋 ▶𒁹 begin with *g*, *c*, or *k*, and does it end with *z*, *s̄*, *ts*, or *s*? Mr. Smith would refer the word to כסה "to conceal," Dr. Delitzsch to Aram. קיסָא "wood," while my own conviction is that it has the same root as קוֹץ "jungle." Variant forms are here almost our sole criterion, and it is only by this means that we can determine that ▶◄ 𒈾 is to be read *tib*, not *tip*, and referred to the root בוא. We shall have to return to this difficulty when dealing with the phonology of the Assyrian language.

APPENDIX TO LECTURE III.

NOTE 1.—Mr. Smith has found a passage in which the name of Gisdhubar is followed by the syllable *ra*, which implies that the name ended in *r*. The reasons Mr. Smith has given for identifying Gisdhubar with Nimrod are very strong; he might have added that the word Nimrod itself may be connected with Marad, the name of the Babylonian town to which Gisdhubar belonged. Sir H. Rawlinson was the first to point out that Gisdhubar was a solar hero, and that the great Babylonian epic in twelve books, which narrated his adventures, was based on the passage of the sun through the twelve signs of the zodiac. The account of the Deluge is introduced as an episode in the eleventh book of the epic, answering to the zodiacal Aquarius.

NOTE 2.—I somewhat doubt the reading Khasis-adra. In the first place, the word or words which Mr. Smith reads thus are found in two passages only, in the first of which the first two characters (*ad-ra*) have to be supplied, and in the second no determinative prefix of a proper name precedes the group of characters in question. Secondly, in both passages (supposing the first is restored correctly) we have *Adra-khasis* not Khasis-adra as the Greek Sisuthrus would require. Thirdly, the name of Tam-zi sometimes has a *tiv* affixed, which looks like a phonetic complement indicating the reading of the name in Assyrian. And fourthly the natural translation of the second passage mentioned above would be :—

adra khasis su-na-ta yu-sap-ri-su.

Then intelligently the dream he caused to explain to him.

4*

Note 3.—Dū-zi, literally "the son of life," came to signify "the only son." He was both son and husband of Istar or Astarte, and in one passage is identified with the Sun-god. It was in pursuit of the dead Dū-zi that Istar descended into Hades. Tam-zi is "the morning sun," that is the sun which rises again after its nightly disappearance and death, and the similarity of the words Dū-zi and Tam-zi, both referring to the same deity, seem to have occasioned the confusion between Du-zu and Tammuz or Adonis in the Semitic languages. See M. Fr. Lenormant, *Sur le nom de Tammouz*, 1876.

LECTURE IV.

The Transmission of the Assyrian Syllabary.

———

I MUST now give some account of the modifications undergone by the Assyrian syllabary in its application to the needs of other languages. We have already seen that it was itself adapted to the wants of a Semitic speech from the characters of a Turanian dialect, and just as it was borrowed by Assyrians and altered to suit their convenience, so it was also borrowed by neighbouring nations, and more or less changed in the process.

Even before what we may call its Assyrian era, that is before the Semites had learned the Accadian system of writing, it was used in the great monarchy of Anzan, or Southern Susiania and its capital Susa. We ought not to forget that it was from this mountainous country of Elam that the Accadians had originally descended, and that several facts, such as the use of papyrus as a writing material, or the ignorance of the palm-tree, go to show that the syllabary had been invented before their arrival in the fertile plains of Chaldea.[1] It was only natural, therefore, that the Susianians should have employed the cuneiform syllabary from an early date, and that the characters should be of the Archaic Babylonian form. It must be observed, however, that they are already cuneiform or wedge-shaped; and this shows that they must have been derived from the Accadians after the latter had learnt to stamp them upon clay, and consequently were not a common heritage which had come down from the period when the Accadians were still in their early mountain home. Chaldea was so often overrun and

---

[1] See Note 1 in the Appendix at the end of the chapter.

conquered by the Elamites that there is nothing astonishing in a community of arts and sciences among them. At present there are but few specimens of Susianian inscriptions in Europe and these are mostly on broken bricks from Susa. M. Lenormant has given copies of all that are known in the second part of his *Choix des Textes Cunéiformes;* and a glance at these will inform us that the type of character is the same as that found on the bricks of the primitive Chaldean kings.

Among the four tribes, however, into which Strabo says the country was divided, that of Anzan or Susa was by far the most civilised; indeed, the others, with the exception of the Cassi or Kossæans, were in a very backward state. The Amardi, in the north-east, spoke the same dialect as the aboriginal Turanian population of Media; and this dialect, the Proto-medic as it is sometimes called, became of such importance in the Persian era, when but insignificant remains were left of the Turanian inhabitants of Anzan and the Magian Medes were exercising a large influence on their Aryan conquerors, as to be made the representative of the languages spoken by the Turanian subjects of Persia. It was necessary, therefore, that they should be provided with a system of writing. This was already in existence among the Amardians, as may be seen from the inscriptions copied by Mr. Layard at Mál Amir, but it had been borrowed from the Assyrians of Nineveh. The Assyrian syllabary had been greatly simplified, polyphones had been rejected, and only a little more than one hundred characters retained, including ideographs. Even the forms of the characters had been made more simple; thus 𒊭 (*sa*), has but three wedges instead of four (𒊭), 𒊓 has become 𒊏 (*rak*), and 𒄯 is written 𒄯 (*khir*). The simplification of form has proceeded to greater length in the Persian period than in that of the Mal Amir inscriptions, and one or two characters used at Mal Amir have been dropped. The number of ideographs employed is very limited, as is also the number of single characters which express a syllable beginning and ending with a consonant.

The Alarodian nations north of Assyria had similarly borrowed the Assyrian syllabary in a modified form, though probably not before the ninth century B.C.[1] The inscriptions copied at Van and its neighbourhood by

[1] See Note 2 in the Appendix at the end of the chapter.

Schulz in 1828 are inscribed in characters identical with those that occur on the monuments of Nineveh, except that a double wedge takes the place of a single line where this passes through another wedge. Thus ⊨ (*pa*), is ⊨⊨ , ⊞ is ⊨⫼⊨ . The Vannic syllabary, like the Protomedic or Amardian, did not admit polyphones (except, as it would seem, in one instance ⊨⏐), and used but very few ideographs. As in Amardian, also, characters that denoted closed syllables were rare; but on the contrary a great and extended use was made of the vowels. Thus we find *a, u, e, u* following one another, and *tar* is followed by *a, i, e.* Dr. Hincks supposed that the final vowels of a syllable were not sounded at the end of words, *par-ri-ni-ni*, for instance, being read *parrinin;* but there are no grounds for this view.

We have thus seen what was the cuneiform mode of writing employed to express the sounds and words of Turanian, Semitic, and Alarodian languages; but we must now consider its final and most remarkable adaptation to the wants of Aryan speakers. If we trace the characters from their pictorial origin through the modifications they underwent in Babylonia, in Assyria, and in Media, we shall see a constant process of simplification. But it was among the Aryan Persians that they attained their highest point of simplification and developed into an alphabet of forty characters, in accordance with the analytic and simplifying tendency of the Aryan mind. M. Oppert[1] has recently shown us how this alphabet was created. One of the significations of a character when used as an ideograph was selected and translated by the corresponding Persian word, and the first letter of the Persian word was assigned to the character as its value in the new alphabet. At the same time all the wedges that could be spared were thrown away, so that the Persian letters are but shadows and maimed relics of the primitive ideographs. Thus ▸⊨⏐◂ "time of life," *zaya* in Persian, is contracted into ▸⏐◂ and given the power of *z (a, u)*; ⟨⊞ "sacrifice," *havana* in Persian, becomes ⟨⊏◂ and stands for *h*. In this way, we can account for the inherent vowels, as they are called, which belonged to the letters of the Persian alphabet. Thus ⏐⊨ is used for *k* before *a* and *i* because it is derived from the Assyrian ⊒ which signified "work," *karta* in Persian, but ⟨⏐ is *k* when followed by *u* because this character comes from the Assyrian ◂⏐, the ideograph of the "sun," which was called *kuru* in

Persian. Besides the letters of the alphabet, the Persians also admitted a few ideographs, which again were shortened forms of the old Assyrian characters. Thus ⟘⟨⟨ *khshatriya* "king," is the Assyrian ⟗ of the same meaning; ⟨⟨⟨⟩ *dahyāva* "countries," is the Assyrian ⟘⟘ or ⟘⟘⟘ *matâti*, "lands." I am not going to say that all the explanations of the Persian alphabet given by M. Oppert can be defended; some of his comparisons are indeed extremely questionable; but in the majority of instances he is undoubtedly correct, and the discovery of the principle upon which the alphabet is based is a triumph of skill and acuteness.

I have now described in brief outline the various phases through which have passed the corrupted forms of the hieroglyphics invented by a Turanian race in the mountains of Elam such long ages ago. The cuneiform system of writing was certainly a clumsy one, even in its last and most perfect development, but it says much for the difficulty of inventing a system of writing at all, and for the debt that civilised man owes to those who did so, that this clumsy system should have lasted so long and been adopted by so many nations and races. When it finally became disused it is not easy to say, but at all events it was not until after the Christian era. Inscriptions in the Assyrian language and in the Assyrian syllabary have been found by Mr. Smith at Babylon dated in the reign of the Parthian king Arsakes. One of these belongs to his second year, and another refers to two eras one Greek and the other Parthian, the 154th of the one, in which the tablet is dated, being called the 208th of the other. As the Greek or Seleucid era counts from B.C. 311, while the Parthian Empire was founded by Arsakes I. in B.C. 247, the date of the tablet will be B.C. 103, in the reign of the Arsakes who is generally known in history by the name of Mithridates II. A still more modern Assyrian inscription has been found by M. Oppert among the antiquities of the Museum at Zürich; and if he is right in identifying the king mentioned upon it with Pakorus, the brother of Vologêses III., the legend will have been inscribed in the age of Domitian. As it is thus of considerable interest, I will reproduce it in full :—

1. *šak-ši*　40　　*bar-sa*　　𒁹　*La-ras-sib*(𒁹⊢)
　　Bill　of 40　half-manehs　　　Larassib,

2. *'ablu*　*sa*　𒁹⊢𒁹　*Bel-akhi-mis-šu*
　　son　of　　　　　of Bel-akhi-erib?

3. *ina eli*　𒁹　*Zir-iddina* (⚒) *'ablu*　*sa*
　　for　　　　Zir-iddin　　　the son of

4. 𒁹𒁹𒁹　*ina*　　*D.P. Airi*　40　　*bar-sa*　　*ina*
　　Ablai　in　the month Iyyar　40　half-manehs　in

5. 　　*Bit*　*Sam-si*　　*E-ci*
　　the temple of the sun　at Babylon

6. *i-nan-din*
　　he gives.

7. 　　*mu-cin*　𒁹　*Ur-ra-me*
　　The witness(es)　Urrame,

8. *'ablu*　*sa*　𒁹　*Pu-a,*　𒁹　*A l*(?)-*lit*(?)
　　son　of　　Pua,　　　Allit(?)

9. *'ablu*　*sa*　𒁹　*Ai-rat*　𒁹　*Ci-is-tar*
　　son　of　　Airat,　　　Cistar

10. *'ablu*　*sa*　𒁹　*Si-nam*
　　son　of　　Sinam.

11. *Zir-iddina*　　*nisu . . .'ablu*　*sa*　𒁹𒁹𒁹
　　Zir-iddin,　the writer　son　of　Ablai

12. *sa*(?)　*E-ci*　　*D.P.*　　*Cisiliv*　*yumu 3* ⊨⊨
　　in　Babylon,　the month　Cisleu,　the third day,

13. *sanatu*　5 *kan*　𒁹 ⊿ -*kha-ri-* 𒁹 (?)
　　the　fifth year　Pi(?)-kha-ri-su

14. *šar*　*mat*　*Pa-ar-su*
　　king　of　Persia.

You will see that unfortunately the name of the king is not absolutely certain. At the same time there is no name among the kings of Parthia and Babylon which will well suit the characters that are certain except that of Pacorus, and the resemblance between ⊿ and ⊨⊢ *pi*, need not be pointed out. If this inscription is really of so late an age as it seems to be, we can easily understand how a native of Babylonia, like Berosus, could have accurately translated into Greek the mythology and history and astronomy of his country. While Pliny was busied in collecting vague and contradictory scraps of information about the ancient astronomy of Chaldea, there were still living men who could have interpreted to him those very astronomical tablets which have lain so long buried under the soil. With characteristic contempt for the languages and culture of other nations, the Romans like the Greeks before them neglected the knowledge which lay at their doors, and left it to the skill and patience of the nineteenth century to decipher the records which throw so precious a light on the history of human civilisation.

APPENDIX TO LECTURE IV.

NOTE I.—As I have pointed out in the *Transactions of the Society of Biblical Archæology*, Vol. I., part 2, pp. 343-45, the ideograph ⊢𝍖, which is used to signify "a written tablet," is really composed of two characters, one denoting "writing" and the other "water." As the Accadian name of the ideograph is *alal* "papyrus," it is plain that papyrus must have been employed as a writing material while the primitive hieroglyphics out of which the cuneiform characters arose were still in the course of formation. M. Oppert long ago remarked that the want of a special ideograph to represent the palm-tree implied that those primitive hieroglyphics had been perfected into a system before the Accadians descended into the alluvial plain of Babylonia. Now it was only after their settlement there that clay could have been employed for writing purposes; we are therefore justified in believing that the use of papyrus preceded the use of clay and that the cuneiform system of writing in its original shape was employed before its inventors had left their mountain home. Pliny (*Nat. Hist.*, xiii. 22) states that the papyrus grew in the Euphrates in the neighbourhood of Babylon and was there used as writing-paper.

NOTE 2.—By the Alarodian nations are meant those populations of Armenia and the neighbouring countries who spoke languages akin to the modern Georgian. These languages are inflectional in character, but cannot be connected with those of the Aryan family. The Assyrian mode of writing seems to have been introduced into Armenia by Lutipri or his son 'Sarduri, king of the Manni or Minni, the modern Van. As 'Sarduri is probably the same as 'Seduri, the Armenian monarch with whom Shalmaneser came into contact in his twenty-seventh campaign (B.C. 832), the date of the introduction of the cuneiform syllabary into the country is fairly well fixed. The inscriptions copied by Schulz record the names of Lutipri, his son 'Sarduri, and his grandson Isbuinis I., and then, after a break, contain the annals of Menuas I. and his four descendants Argistis, 'Sarduri II., Isbuinis II. and Menuas II. Argistis was the opponent of Sargon, whose inscriptions inform us that he was preceded on the throne of Van by a king called Ursa, probably an elder brother. It is not until the eighth century B.C. that we find Aryan tribes settling in Armenia. Their proper names as found in the Assyrian inscriptions prove them to have belonged to the Iranian section of the Aryan family and consequently to have formed part of that wave of population which brought the Aryan Medes into Media and the Aryan Persians into Susiania.

LECTURE V.

Assyrian Phonology.

AS the primary object of these lectures is a practical one, I shall confine myself in this and the following to the general outlines and main characteristics of Assyrian grammar, reserving points of detail and disputed questions for a future occasion. For the same reason I shall adopt the arrangement of an ordinary Aryan grammar, taking phonology, nouns and pronouns, verbs, particles, and syntax, according to the order with which Latin and Greek have made us familiar. What has been said on the subject of the Syllabary will have made it plain that Assyrian phonology is by no means an easy matter. Where we have a borrowed system of writing in which the same characters have to do duty for *m* and *v*, for ב and ר, for ז and צ, while final consonants are undistinguished, accurate and trustworthy decisions upon delicate questions of pronunciation can only be reached after long and laborious induction. Upon some points, indeed, it is almost hopeless ever to expect a thoroughly satisfactory conclusion. Such a point is the Assyrian pronunciation and interchange of *m* and *v*. Were these letters kept distinct in pronunciation and only confused in writing, or had the Assyrians under the influence of their Accadian neighbours adopted a sound intermediate between *m* and *v*? In certain cases the latter really seems to have been the case, especially at the beginning of a word; but in other instances such a view is out of the question. Thus, on the one side, *b* before the copulative conjunction is assimilated as in *eruv-va* "he went down, and" for *erub-va*, and here the *v* or *w* sound can alone be admitted; on the other side, grammatical considerations oblige us to assume *m* in the case of the mimmation; and the frequent change of the doubtful letter into *n* before sibilants, dentals, and gutturals, shows that here again it must have been *m*. So far the facts are pretty clear. But now verbs which are ע״ו in Hebrew are written in Assyrian with the equivocal characters which may be read either *m* or *v*: which of these are we to adopt? Are we to read *acmu'* " I burned," *amaru* " to see," or *acvu*, *avaru ?* There is much to be said on both sides; but when we consider the transcription of Merodach and *mana* (*maneh*) in Greek and Hebrew, or of *mannuci* in the Phœnician bilingual legends, to say nothing of the numerous roots in which Assyrian *m* answers to *m* in the cognate dialects, or the equivalence of the Assyrian *Elamu* and *Elum* (fr. עלה) to עילם, it is better to regard the first pronunciation with *m* as more accurately representing the sound of the original. Nothing indeed can be stronger than עילם = עלה where Assyrian must have changed a *v* (for *u*) into *m*, and the case becomes still clearer when we find *m* assimilated to the following consonant in words like *ikhkhar* " he received," *takhkhatsu* " battle," for the usual *imkhar*, *tamkhatsu*, where *m* has first become *n*. We shall see hereafter that one of the distinguishing characteristics of the Babylonian dialect was its retention of the mimmation at the end of nouns and verbs; and hence when we come to a word like 𒀊𒉏𒈠 *ab-num-ma* " I built, and " in an inscription of Nebuchadrezzar it is better to assume that the *v* or *w* of the conjunction has been assimilated by the preceding mimmation, or rather lost altogether, the second *m* expressing only the accent of the preceding syllable. This loss of *v*, through a preceding vocalisation, is of frequent occurrence in the inscriptions. Like the Hebrew copulative conjunction, the Assyrian *va* " and," often appears as *û* simply, and at the end of a verbal form may be dropped altogether. *Sukalula*, for instance, stands for *sukalul-va*, just as *dhābu* " good," stands for *dhăvăbu* (טוב), the *v* being first vocalised and then wholly disappearing. This disappearance of *v* is more common in Assyrian than in Babylonian, so that if a case like that mentioned above occurred on an Assyrian inscription we should rather read *abnuv-va* than *abnumm-a*, regarding the first *v* as simply indicating that the accent lay upon the preceding vowel.

I have dwelt thus long on the changes and interchanges of *m* and *v* because they illustrate so well the difficulties inherent in the subject of Assyrian phonology, and also meet us upon the very threshold of our enquiries. We must now turn to the other chief points to be noticed in the phonetic system of the Assyrians. Let us first take the vowels. *A* may be a vowel as well as a consonant, and here again the cuneiform mode of writing makes no distinction between the two cases. ⟨cuneiform⟩ denotes a syllable in *ta-'a-ru* "to return," merely a long vowel in *khar-sa-ā-nu* "forests." Sometimes, however, *h* (⟨cuneiform⟩) with or without *a* (⟨cuneiform⟩) is introduced when the character is intended to be consonantal. The sound originally expressed by the character has not been exempt from the phonetic decay which has attacked all the less persistent sounds of Assyrian. The original consonantal א may not only lose its breathing but be still further weakened to *i;* and this weakening of *a* into *i* is to be remembered as it forms a characteristic feature of Assyrian. Before or after *u*, *a* is lost altogether. *A + 'a* or *aya* passed into *ai* and accordingly is always used for this diphthong in the inscriptions. Hence *aabu* must be read *aibu* (אוֹיֵב) "wicked," "enemy," not *aabu* as Mr. Smith gives it in his syllabary opposite the Accadian ⟨cuneiform⟩ "a sorcerer," and the gentilic adjective as we shall see ends in *ai* not *aya*, in full accordance with the habit of the other Semitic languages. I have already stated that just as *ha* became *a*, so *va* became *u;* but there is one other observation to be made in regard to this latter vowel. Here again the deficiencies of the old Accadian script make themselves felt, and the same character (⟨cuneiform⟩) was employed for both *u* (= אוּ) and *yu*. Thus it comes about that the first and third persons singular of those conjugations of which *u* is a characteristic are expressed by the same character though pronounced differently. The vowel *i* also may be weakened from the consonantal *ya*. Thus the third singular of the aorist Kal of verbs is always *ispur*, though originally *yaspur*. So *bitu* "house," is also given as *biyatu*, where *y* replaces a primitive *v* after its corresponding vowel *i*. But what distinguishes Assyrian phonology more especially is the close connection that exists between this vowel *i* and *'ayin*. The two sounds are repeatedly interchanged, and where Assyrian weakens *ha* to *i*, Babylonian generally has ע. So completely had a guttural pronunciation of the latter letter been lost that the Assyrian scribe had to represent the initial of the Heb. עַזָּה, Gaza, by *kh*. It was treated in all respects as a mere vowel, falling away in the Assyrian dialect after *u* or before *a*. On the other hand, a reminiscence of its origin was preserved in Babylonian, and to a slight extent in Assyrian. As just stated,

where Assyrian has *i* for *'a*, Babylonian prefers *e*, and this is also the case
where *kh* has been lost. If the lost *kh* is initial, however, Assyrian sometimes represents it by *e* (e.g., *ecilu* הֵכָל " place "). But even in Assyrian verbs
which contain *ayin* generally mark its presence, if possible.

The loss of *kh*, to which I have just referred, is common enough in
Assyrian. Thus *'imiru* is חמור, *ruku* רחק, *pitu* פתח. After a sibilant the
vulgar pronunciation could assimilate the *kheth* following : thus we have
sazzaru for *saskharu* and *sisseru* for *siskhiru* " small." Where *kh* was retained,
however, it might be doubled like *r*. In certain cases *kh* is weakened from
c. When *kh* was thus lost, it was natural that the weaker *h* should suffer the
same fate. In *âlu* " city " for *ahalu* (אהל) and *nâru* " river," for *naharu*
(*nahru*) it has disappeared altogether. In the Persian period we find a
final *h* added to the third person plural of the verb like the quiescent ה of
Arabic.

The Assyrian gutturals, as a general rule, answer to the corresponding
gutturals of Hebrew; ק, however, is often weakened to *caph*, and this again in
some rare examples to ה in the middle of a word. In Babylonian *g* commonly takes the place of ק (as also in later Assyrian) ; while, on the other
hand, roots which contain ג and ז in Hebrew frequently have the stronger
sounds ק and צ in Assyrian. As regards the labials *m* has already been
discussed, and I need only add here that a double *b* or *p* may be replaced by
mb or *mp*, just as a double dental by *nd* or *nt*. The nasal by the way is
generally assimilated to the following letter : but this rule is by no means
invariable.

The dentals are involved in much confusion through the deficiencies of
the syllabary in the matter of *dh*. After a guttural, *t* servile may change into
this sound, and after a nasal into *d*. A preceding *d*, *dh*, *z*, *s*, *ts*, or *s* causes
the assimilation of a servile *t* following, only *st* becomes not *ss* but *ss*. Conversely *t* + *s* becomes *s*, *kat-su* " his hand," for instance, being written *ka-su*.
The sibilants alone now remain. ז, ס, צ, and שׁ were all represented in
Assyrian, but as I tried to show in a previous lecture the Assyrian here again
found a difficulty in adapting a foreign syllabary to the Semitic alphabet.
One character had to stand for *za* and *tsa*, and it is possible that the tendency
to soften *ts* into *z* which we observe in Assyrian, especially in the Babylonian
dialect, was partly due to Accadian influence. The characters which had

represented in Accadian the hissing sound of the Hungarian *sz* were appropriated to the expression of the Semitic *samech*. As *samech* became ξ in Greek while *t + s* was represented by *ś* in Assyrian, it is clear that the pronunciation of the letter must have been sharp. In course of time, however, it became more and more assimilated to simple *s*; thus we find *sarru* by the side of *śarru* "king," *tasbusu* as a variant of *tasbusu*, and (in Babylonian) *usalbis-śu* "I covered it," for *usalbis-su*. The preference of the Babylonian dialect for the softer *s* is analogous to the fact which is brought out in the account embodied in Judges xii. 6, where the northern Israelites (like the Assyrians) were distinguished from their southern brethren by the substitution of *ś* for *s*. The aspirated *s*, however, was unknown just as in the Phœnician alphabet, no distinction being made between *sin* and *shin*. But phonetic decay was setting in against the harsher sibilants, especially in the Babylonian dialect where *ts* is frequently replaced by *z*, and *ś* more rarely so. Thus as far back as the inscription of Khammuragas (before the sixteenth century B.C.) *tsirraśina* (= *tsirrat-sina*) is written *tsirrazina*. In the northern dialect of Assyria, however, the same process of softening had begun. Thus we meet with *arzip* by the side of *artsip* "I built," and *makhazu* by the side of *makhatsu* "slaughter;" and *ts* before *t* regularly became *s*. This softening of the sibilant led to one of the most characteristic marks of Assyrian, a mark which it is impossible to discover in any of the other Semitic dialects; I mean the change of a sibilant into *l* before a dental. This change can only be explained by supposing a prior change into *r*, such as meets us in Latin, and throws some light on the pronunciation of *r*. But just as the nasal though usually assimilated to the following letter was not necessarily so, the mutation of the sibilant into *l* was not always observed. The converse change of *l* into *s*, it must be borne in mind, never took place; and this phonetic fact alone disposes of the theory that the Kaldai of the inscriptions, the Χαλδαῖοι of the Greeks, had any connection with the Casdim of the Old Testament.[1]

Before leaving the subject of phonology, something must be said regarding long vowels, double letters, and the accent. A long vowel was properly expressed by writing the vowel in question after a character with a corresponding inherent vowel: thus *bā* would be written *ba-a*. As before observed, however,

---

[1] See Note 1 in the Appendix at the end of the chapter.

the second vowel might denote a new syllable, while it frequently happens
that the second character is not given at all and the length of the vowel is
left to the knowledge of the reader.   An Assyrian, of course, would experience
little difficulty from this defective mode of writing, since he would know where
a long vowel was to be supplied even when the writing furnished no indication;
but the case is different with us, and in instances of this kind we can only
determine whether or not the vowel is long by a comparison of passages and
an acquaintance with the principles of Assyrian grammar.   The same has to
be said of double letters.   These are as frequently left unexpressed as
expressed, and then, as in Ethiopic, the omission has to be supplied from our
knowledge of the grammar and lexicon.   But a further complication is introduced by the fact that when a double letter is written it may not denote a
double letter at all, but only that the preceding syllable has the accent upon
it.   It may also point out the length of the preceding syllable provided the
accent fall upon it.   The reduplication of a consonant was the sole means the
Assyrians possessed of marking the accent.   The rules of accentuation,
indeed, were simple enough, as in Arabic; the accent being thrown as far
back as possible, that is to say upon the antepenult, unless the penult was a
closed syllable or had a long vowel.   The consequence of this was that when
a word consisted of three short syllables, the second vowel was generally
dropped, making the first a closed syllable.   Enclitics of all kinds, however,
threw the accent upon the preceding syllable, even though that were short
while the syllable before it was long; thus we have *illicŭniv-va* (for *illicuni'-va*)
" they had gone, and;" *ikhdhŭninni* (for *ikhdhuni'-ni*) " they had sinned against
me."   We must account in a similar manner for a form like *uctanna-su* " I
establish it," for *uctána-su*.[1]

The use and formation of the nouns resemble what we find in the other
Semitic dialects.   Substantives and adjectives are distinguished syntactically
only, and possess but two genders, masculine and feminine.   There is no
separate form for the comparative and the superlative, and an article is
equally unknown.   A considerable proportion of the nouns were borrowed
from the Accadians, and one of the chief difficulties of decipherment has
arisen from our ignorance of the meaning of the numerous words so derived
which are not to be found in any of the other Semitic tongues.   Indeed some

See Note 2 in the Appendix at the end of the chapter.

acquaintance with the old language of Chaldea is absolutely necessary for a full understanding of Assyrian itself.

For details as to the formation of verbal nouns I must refer to my *Assyrian Grammar*. Here, in accordance with the practical plan and scope of the present lectures, I can only set before you those general outlines which are indispensable as an introduction to a scientific study of Assyrian grammar. As in the other Semitic dialects we must distinguish between primitive nouns and those derived from the various forms of the verb. The latter are numerous enough. For the present, however, it is necessary for us to fix our attention upon two or three only. First and foremost a careful distinction must be made between two forms which are very frequently written alike in the inscriptions, though the meanings they bear differ widely. *Málicu* "ruling," with a long or accented *â*, and *malicu* "king," with a short *a*, are generally written in the same way; but the one is a *nomen agentis* or participle, the other a *nomen permanentis*. Both forms again have to be kept apart from a third *malicu* "ruled over," the *nomen mutati*, with a long *i*, though this is often left unmarked on the monuments. Similarly we have to distinguish between the *nomen permanentis sacan*, with the second syllable short, and the *nomen mutationis* or infinitive *sacan*, with the second syllable long. The first form regularly loses its second vowel before the case-endings, as in *kardu* for *karadu*, the second form never. Other forms of less importance to distinguish between are also written alike, while forms derived from Pael which properly double the second consonant are not unfrequently met with written defectively.

Nouns, however, formed by vowel change or the doubling of a radical make up but a small part of the numerous verbal derivatives with which we meet. The latter are created by the help of extraneous letters and syllables, the origin of which is still a subject of enquiry. Corresponding with the Niphal conjugation we have a number of words, with more or less a passive signification, formed by prefixing a nasal. Thus from בחר "to choose," we get *nabkharu* "chosen," from בנה "to create," *nabnitu* "offspring." To the causative Shaphel, again, answer words like *satsu*, "expulsion," from יצא "to go out," *sumkutu*, "slaughter," from מקת. The conjugations with *t* inserted, Iphteal, Iphtaal, etc., have analogous nouns, *kitrubu* "a meeting," from קרב, *gitmalu* "a benefactor," from גמל. Equally common are the forms which prefix the dental, such as *tasmeatu* " hearing," from שמע. You will notice the preservation of *ayin* in this word; in a verbal form the *a* would have absorbed it, and we should have had *tasmâtu*. From the same root we get *Tasmitu* the name of Nebo's wife, of whom Assur-bani-pal tells us that they had enlarged his ears and sharpened his sight so that he had all the characters of the syllabary as many as existed written down and stored in his palace for the inspection of his people. As Nebo or Nabiu signified "the prophet," or "proclaimer," so the name of "the hearer" was appropriately given to his consort. The first syllable of her name is written 𒌷 and was long read *Ur*, an instance at once of the difficulties attendant on the decipherment of the inscriptions and of the successful removal of these difficulties by a knowledge of the structure of the language. The reading *Urmitu* would show no Assyrian root. Another example of the determination of a reading by a philological knowledge of the language is afforded by the word which means "a coping," and is often transliterated *gablubu*. This however, would require a quadriliteral root, and such are not very common in Assyrian, whereas by adopting *takh*, another value of 𒀀, we get *takhlupu*, a *t* formation from the common root חלף "to cover." Two very common words on the historical monuments, *tamkharu* and *tamkhatsu* are again instances of the same formation. They both signify "battle," the first coming from the root מחר "to be present," and so properly meaning "opposition," a "facing one another," and the other from מחץ "to slay." As before remarked the *m* after passing into a nasal may be assimilated to the following guttural, and then written defectively; so that instead of *tamkharu* and *tamkhatsu* we sometimes meet with *takharu* and *takhatsu*. Of course when the root begins with 'ayin or aleph *ta* becomes *te*, as in the abstract *tenisetu* "mankind," from אנוש. In verbs פ״ן we find *tu*.

Another way of forming a derivative is by prefixing a vowel. Traces of this kind of formation are to be met with in the Old Testament, in the name of Isaac "the laugher," from צחק, for instance, but it is by no means uncommon in Assyrian. The vowel was originally *a* or *yā*, but in course of time it became weakened into *i* and even *u;* and so we find *alcacat* "histories," by the side of *ilcacat*. In a so-called biliteral root, that is a root in which one of the three component letters has become a vowel, the initial consonant is often doubled to show the length of the prefixed vowel. Thus besides *miru* "youngling," we have *immiru*, where the first syllable is both long and accented.

One of the most frequently used of the external formatives is *m* which is employed to denote the instrument, action or place, as well as to form the participles of the derived conjugations. Here, again, the vowel which originally followed *m* was *a*, which however, has been weakened to *i* and *ŭ*. Thus in the epigraphs of the Black Obelisk we read the word *ma-da-at-tu* "tribute." *Madattu* stands for *maddattu* and that again for *mandattu* and *mandantu* from the root נדן "to give," so that the word properly signifies "that which is given." Whenever this suffix *m* is used to form the present participle of the derived conjugation of the verb, it has the vowel *u* after it: thus *munassiku* "the biter," the name of one of Assur-bani-pal's dogs.

We have not yet finished with the derivatives which could be created by the addition of new letters. A large number of abstracts and adjectives used as substantives are made by affixing the termination *-ānu* which rarely became *-īnu* (or *innu*) and *-ūnu*. These correspond to similar words in Hebrew which end in *-ôn*: the Assyrian *lisānu* "tongue," for example, is the Hebrew *lâshôn*, and originally signified "the licker;" *sildhanu* "king," is the Aramaic *shildhôn*, the *sultân* of modern days; and *kirbanu* "offering," from קרב "to approach," or "bring near," is the Hebrew *kŏrbân*, Arabic *kurbân* of which we read in the New Testament. It is a curious instance of the way in which words travel about that the name under which the sea-kelp goes in the Channel Islands is *korban*, a reminiscence of a pious Puritan age which saw in the chief sustenance of a starving peasantry a *korban* or "gift" from God. This termination in *-ānu*, however, was really at the outset nothing but the plural, and the words so formed were collectives which gradually came to lose all their plural force and meaning. So just as the Romance nations forgot that the Latin *maria, studia* were neuter plurals and came to regard them as feminine singulars (*la mer, l'étude*) like *musa*, the Assyrians like the Hebrews forgot the origin of this termination in *-ân*, and looking upon it as simply expressive of the idea of the abstract, provided it with feminine and plural endings. ´Thus from *alma(tu)*, "a forsaken one," was formed *almân* "forsaken ones," i.e., "forsakeness," and from that again we get in the inscriptions *almānătu* "a widow," *almānātu*, (Heb. *'almânâh*) "widows." A similar fate has befallen another termination which is employed to build abstracts. This is -*utu*, as in *sarrutu* "a kingdom," from *sarru*. As we shall see, this has exactly the same form as the suffix of certain masculine plurals, the only distinction between them being that of meaning and use: the abstracts in -*ūtu* were always feminine, like all other abstract nouns, and never admitted the plural.

There are two other nominal formations of which it is necessary to take note, as they frequently occur in the inscriptions and may at first sight somewhat puzzle the student. They both belong to those defective or biliteral roots in which one or more of the three component consonants is liable to become vocalised. Roots which begin with א or ו have curious derived forms which repeat the second radical; thus from *alacu* "to go," we get *liliccu* "a going." One of the words which illustrate this formation is *dadmi* "men," which stands by the side of *adamu* or *admu*, the Hebrew *âdâm*, and is interesting as being one of the radicals which show the close connection between the Assyrian and Hebrew lexicons, this particular word being found only in Hebrew, Phœnician, Assyrian and Himyaritic, and not in any of the other Semitic idioms. We sometimes meet with the phrase *ana pakad kal dadmi* "to superintend all men;" and it is a striking instance of the impossibility of arriving at a satisfactory decipherment of the inscriptions without a full knowledge of the peculiarities of Assyrian grammar, that M. Ménant in one of the translations appended to his *Grammaire Assyrienne*, written in the early days of Assyriology, transcribed the sentence *ana pakad kalda admi*, and so obtained the unhistorical and equally ungrammatical rendering "to superintend the men of the Chaldeans." The other nominal formation from defective roots to which I wish to call your attention is one from roots which begin with *n*, *a* or *u* (Heb. י). In all these cases the first syllable is dropped: and so we have *sahu* "summit," and *sas'u* (for *sass'u*) "spoil," from נשא; *radu* or *ridu* "servant," *rittu* (for *rid(ĭ)tu*) "foot," and the passive *rudu* "chariot," from ירד "to go down;" and *lidu* or *littu* (for *lid(ĭ)tu*) "offspring," from ילד "to bear." From the same radix we get *lidanu* "offspring," with the termination in -*ānu* on which I dwelt just now.

I must now speak of the cases of the noun; for Assyrian like Arabic preserved the three cases which were originally possessed by all the Semitic languages. These cases ended in -*u* for the nominative, -*i* for the genitive, and -*a* for the accusative, and had once been kept clearly distinct. At the epoch, however, to which our earliest Assyrian monuments mount back this clear consciousness of their distinction had been lost and a tendency had set in to use these cases one for the other, the accusative and genitive being employed for the nominative and *vice versâ*. The later the age of the inscription, the more frequent does this misuse of the cases become, although to the last the distinction between them was never wholly forgotten, and accurate writers like the scribes of Assur-bani-pal took care not to confuse them. The vowel-ending -*i* came to have the preponderance, partly through its being a weakened form of both *a* and *u*, partly through the influence of the prevailing plural termination in -*i*. We learn from comparative philology that all these case-endings were originally long although the later inscriptions almost invariably make them short; and that there was a time when only the objective termination in -*a* existed, -*i* and -*u* having been subsequently developed out of it. Here is another illustration of the lesson taught us by the science of language that the object historically precedes the subject, the objective case the subjective. But the Assyrian case-endings were distinguished by a further peculiarity, which has been lost by all the other Semitic languages with the exception of one dialect of the Himyaritic inscriptions. This peculiarity is a terminal *m*, which closed in the vowel, and was probably pronounced much in the same way as that final *m* in Latin which could be elided before a vowel. Instead of *m*, Arabic has *n* in the same place, and as this nasal termination goes by the name of nunnation, the similar phenomenon in Assyrian has been termed mimmation. *M* was older than *n* since we elsewhere find final *m* in the Semitic tongues becoming *n*, in the sign of the plural for instance, just as in Greek a terminal *m* changes into the nasal. The mimmation came to be more and more omitted in Assyrian, and we often come across inscriptions in which it is absent altogether, while in others its use is extremely irregular. The southern dialect of Babylonia was far more conservative than the northern dialect of Assyria in this particular respect. Up to the last the Babylonian inscriptions are characterised by a frequent employment of the mimmation, and while the presence of it is exceptional in Assyrian, the omission of it is exceptional in Babylonian. As we shall see, the mimmation is found in verbs as well as in nouns, and its existence explains the primitive length of the case-vowels.

As in the other Semitic idioms, the genitive relation is ordinarily denoted by that close connection of the governed and governing words which allowed them both to be pronounced like a sort of compound in one breath, and shortened the form of the first or governing noun. This shortening is effected in Assyrian in a very simple way, by dropping the case-endings and mimmation of the first word, and attaching the genitive termination in -*i* to the second. Thus from *ziciru* (Heb. *zécer*) or *zicirum* " memory," we get *zicir sumi* " memory of the name," *zicir sarruti* " memory of the sovereignty." Surd roots lose the last syllable and with that the last radical, as *sar* from *sarru*. The shortened form is the one invariably assumed by the construct genitive, so that whenever we meet with cases like *belutu Assur* " lordship of Assur," we may be quite sure that we have to do with two nouns not in the genitive relation but in apposition to one another, so that the literal rendering of the clause would be " the lordship, viz., Assur." Besides this construct genitive, the Assyrians made increasing use of a periphrastic genitive, with the relative pronoun *sa* " which " placed between the first noun with the case-ending of the nominative and the second noun with the case-ending of the genitive. Thus instead of *zicir sumi* we might have *ziciru sa sumi*, literally " the memorial which (belongs to) the name," and so " the memorial of the name," *sa* coming by degrees to have the force of a mere preposition " of," like the Greek χάριν " because of."

There were but two genders in Assyrian, masculine and feminine, abstracts being included under the latter. Many feminine substantives have no distinctive termination, and their gender can only be known from their meaning, plural form, or employment with feminine adjectives, like *'ummu* " mother," *uznu* " ear," *lisanu* " tongue." Those that have a distinctive suffix are of three kinds. (1) Feminine abstracts in *ūtu* already mentioned. (2) The general feminine ending in -*ătu* (e.g., *napsatu*, *belat*, contracted *beltu*, *pulkhatu*, *pulukhtu*.) (3) In -*ĭtu* weakened from -*ătu* (thus both *belatu* and *belitu*; *binitu* and *bintu*). The latter was the only form admitted in roots ל"ע.

Assyrian possessed a dual as well as a plural, though its use was confined to a few words which denoted pairs like *uznā* " the ears," *katā* " the hands," *sepā* " the feet." These examples will show that it was expressed by the termination *ā*. The plural was formed in several ways. The oldest was that in -*ānu*, etc., which was used indiscriminately for both masculine and feminine substantives (e.g., feminines *emukānu*, "powers," *risānu* "heads.") Sometimes, however, we find feminine nouns which have not only this but also the more modern plural termination in -*ātu*, as e.g., *pānu* or *pātu* "faces." Sometimes, again, masculines which have adopted the later masculine ending are occasionally met with under the form -*ānu*. Instead of -*ānu*, the weakened form *āni* is usually found apparently through the influence of the common plural in -*i* (e.g., *kharsāni* "forests," *duppāni*, "tablets"). Just as the original case-ending -*a* was softened into *u*, so besides -*ānu* there is a rare form -*ūnu* which occurs in the word *dilūnu* "buckets," and a few others.

But besides *dilunu*, there was another plural *dilūtu*, which furnishes us with an instance of a very common Assyrian plural in -*ūtu*. It was set apart for masculine nouns, though the fact that a precisely similar formation denoted feminine abstracts singular shows that it was properly and primarily the characteristic of feminine nouns. How it came to be restricted to the opposite gender is an example of a phenomenon that frequently occurs in the history of language. It was the form of the plural adopted for all adjectives and present participles, as well as for roots ל״ה, etc.

The ordinary plural of masculine substantives was, however, one in -*i* or -*e*. This resembles the construct masculine plural in Hebrew, and like the latter has lost a final *m* or *n*. But whereas Hebrew confined this contracted form to the construct genitive, Assyrian applied it to all cases alike, thus giving another illustration of its liability to phonetic decay. The result of this was that in many nouns it is impossible to distinguish between the plural and the genitive singular, both being pronounced alike, though an attempt was sometimes made, especially in Babylonian, to keep them apart in writing by using *e* instead of *i* for the plural. This was the easier from the fact that the vowel of the plural was when correctly sounded longer than that of the genitive singular, the long vowel of the latter having been worn away before the action of decay had begun to break down the plural termination. Another mode of distinguishing between the two forms was adopted in the case of dissyllables, when the accent was on the first syllable and the second syllable was short, by dropping the vowel of the second syllable in the singular, and retaining it in the plural, of course accenting it at the same time. Thus *nácri* is "enemy," (genitive singular), *nacíri* "enemies," *nakhli* "valley," *nakhalli* (for *nakháli*) "valleys." But in other words the confusing consequences of phonetic decay are as conspicuous as in our own "sheep," and the context or grammar alone can determine whether the word is singular or plural. When we meet, for instance, with a sentence like *rabbi bitu* we may know at once that *rabbi* here must be the plural, since the law which regulates the construct genitive would require *rab bitu*, were it in the singular. It may be remarked that besides this plural in -*e* many nouns also retain the earlier plural in -*ānu* (e.g., *sarrānu* by the side of *sarri*).

In opposition to the masculine plural in -*i* there is the feminine plural in -*ātu* (-*āti*, -*āta*), which is sometimes weakened to -*ītu* or *ētu*, especially in the case of adjectives used as substantives (e.g., *esreti* "sacred places," perhaps connected with the Hebrew '*ashērah*). Many substantives are of common gender, and therefore admitted of both the masculine and feminine plural, like *babu* "gate," which has the two plurals *babi* and *babātu*. This fact will suggest a solution of the curious phenomenon I alluded to just now, the restriction, namely, of what was originally the feminine plural to masculine nouns.

The Assyrian cardinal numerals, as in the other Semitic languages, have two forms, one feminine and the other masculine, but those from 3 to 10 use the masculine with feminine nouns and the feminine with masculine nouns. This, again, is another illustration of the transition of meaning in what was primarily the feminine form of plural nouns. In old Babylonian, however, we find traces of a different and more correct usage, where besides *ciprātu irbái* "the four zones," we have *tupukātu irbittu* with the same meaning. The larger number of the cardinals are met with on the monuments; only those in brackets in my *Elementary Assyrian Grammar* are still un-detected. Their conjectural restoration, however, is pretty certain. Instead of writing each number in full, the Assyrians generally made use of a symbolical mode of expressing them like our ciphers. In this system, an upright wedge (𒁹) denoted 1, two upright wedges (𒐈) 2, and so on. For 4, instead of writing the wedges one after the other, three were written in one line and one beneath, thus 𒃻; and the same arrangement was adopted as far as 7, when a third line was added (𒐛). For 9, there was besides 𒐙 the abbreviation 𒐉. Ten was expressed by 𒌋, and the succeeding numerals were denoted by the help of this arrow-head and the wedge. Thus 11 was ⟨𝕀, 15 ⟨𝕎, 20 ⟨⟨, and so on. With 60, however, a new system begins which is at first sight somewhat puzzling. The Accadians had attained to remarkable mathematical proficiency, and had found that the duodécimal was scientifically a more convenient numerical system than the decimal, the only recommendation of which is that it is the first suggested to the savage by the fact of his possessing ten fingers. They consequently made 60 their unit, and accordingly in the development of their arithmetical symbols represented both 1 and 60 in the same way by the upright wedge. It is sometimes difficult, therefore, to determine whether 1 or 60 is intended in the inscriptions; indeed this can frequently be done only by the help of the context or internal probability. The wedge for 60, however, was generally thicker and larger than that for 1. After 60 there is no difficulty, since the combinations 𝕀𝕀, 𝕀𝕀𝕀, 61, 62, etc., and 𝕀⟨, 𝕀⟨⟨ 70, 80, etc., are not otherwise met with. For 100 the character ⊢ *me* was employed, since *me* in Accadian signified " multitude," and then " one hundred," in which sense it was borrowed by the Semites. 1000 was easily expressed by prefixing ⟨ (10) to the sign for 100.

A noun in the masculine plural always follows the cardinals, as *esritu alpi* " 10 oxen ;" in the case of weights and measures, arithmetical terms, etc., however, the noun is put in the singular, thus *esri mana* " 10 manehs." In the latter instance the measure is often preceded by the preposition *ina* " by," followed by the sign of unity, but without any change of meaning : cc *ina* 1. *ammat* (⊨𝕀𝕀𝕀⊨ 𝕀⟨⟨), for example, being literally " 200 × 1 (i.e., 200) cubits."

The ordinals were formed from the cardinals, with the exception of the terms for " first " *ristānu*, from *risu* " head," and *makhru* " foremost." Thus " second " was *sannu*, feminine *sannutu* (with *nn* for *ny*, i.e., *nw*), " third " was *salsu*, feminine *salistu*. A formation similar to *ristanu* denoted relations of time, thus *saniy-ānu* was " the second time," *salsi-y-ānu* " third time," etc. Collectives took the form *sunnu* " a pair," plural *sunne*, *sulsu* " a triplet," etc.

The names of the fractions, on the other hand, seem to have been derived from the Accadians, although the forms just mentioned, *sulsu*, *rubu*, etc., appear to have been sometimes applied to this purpose. Thus *sussānu* was " a third," from the Accadian *sussana*, *sinibu* " two-thirds," from Accadian *sanabi*, *parapu* " five-sixths," *baru* or *māsu* " one-half." This is another illustration of the borrowed nature of the mathematical knowledge of the Assyrians, who had to take even their name for the mathematical unit, the *soss* (60), from Accadian. So too *saros* (3600) and *ner* (600, symbolised by ⟨⟨ which also equals 70) are of Accadian origin.

Indeed it will be found on closer inspection that most of the names of weights and measures came like the syllabary from the Turanian predecessors of the Semitic population in Western Asia. Thus the standard of length, the *casbu* (7 miles), pl. *casbume*, is an Accadian word derived from *kas* "two," and *bu* " length," and from being a measure of length it came to be used as a measure of time. In this case two of our hours went to make up 1 *casbu*, and some of the astronomical reports, sent in to the king from the observatories of Assyria, mentioned that at the vernal equinox day and night were equal (*sitkulu*), there being 6 *casbu* of the day and 6 of the night. Other astronomical terms had a similar Accadian origin, since this science also, together with the formation of a Calendar and the division of the year, owed its beginning to that ancient people. From them, too, came another word, which after being applied to the valuation of money, and passing through the vocabularies of Greece and Rome, is still preserved in our dictionary. This is the *maund* or *maneh*, the μνᾶ of the Greeks, the *mina* of the Romans, which appears in its most primitive form *mana* in the Accadian column of an ancient table of laws. Already at that remote date it was employed to measure the precious metals, and so would be readily taken up by the Semites, those merchants of the old world. Through them it made its way to Egypt and at a later period to the nations of Europe, and still remains an enduring monument of the debt which civilisation owes to the forgotten thinkers of Chaldea.

APPENDIX TO LECTURE V.

NOTE 1.—The land of Kaldu or Caldu is first mentioned by Assur-natsir-pal (col. iii. 24.) in B.C. 878, and in B.C. 850 his son Shalmaneser speaks of the district as lying below Babylonia on the Persian Gulf (Obelisk 83). It was not till a later period that the Caldai occupied Babylonia, and under Merodach-Baladan made themselves so important and integral a part of its population as to give their names to the whole country. The word Casdim is best explained by the Assyrian root *casadu* "to possess," or "conquer," so that the Casdim will be those Semitic "conquerors" who first settled in Sumir or Shinar, and finally succeeded in extirpating the power and the language of their Accadian predecessors.

NOTE 2.—The following exceptions to the general rule of Assyrian accentuation may be noticed :

(1) The enclitic -*va* threw back its accent upon the preceding syllable, as remarked in the text.

(2) The possessive· pronouns of the first, second, and third persons when suffixed to a noun threw the accent back upon the preceding syllable, as *panú-ca* " thy face," *ramanú-su* " himself," *ramanú-sun* " themselves."

(3) The possessive pronoun suffixes of the verb, with the exception of the second plural and third masculine singular, threw the accent back upon the preceding syllable, as *rasib-á-ni* " pierce me," *itticruh-á-ni* "they were estranged from me," *tucassipí-ni* " thou (fem.) didst reveal to me," *pitá-si* " open for her." A double accent is even permitted in *icsudá-sú-va* " he conquered him, and."

(4) The vowel between the first and second radical was accented in the present of Kal, as *isácin, isácinu.* So, too, in the quadriliteral *iparásid.*

(5) The penult was accented in the third plural masculine, and perhaps

also feminine, as *itsbútu* "they seized," *immáru* "they were visible," *itúru* "they returned."

(6) The penult was accented in the present Kal of verbs ל״ע, as *iséri* from סרע and *isísi* from שׁסע.

(7) The third person singular of the subjective aorist ot Kal and Niphal was accented on the penult, as *ippisídu* "it was alleged," *inúkhu* "it had rested."

(8) Dissyllabic nouns whose first syllable was accented, the second syllable being short, accented the second syllable in the plural, as *nakháli* "valleys," *nacíri* "enemies," in contradistinction to the genitive singular *nákhli* and *nácri*.

(9) Certain nouns accented the penult, like *agúru* "cement," *citstsílu* "royal," *barzílu* "iron," *cidínu* "ordinance," *cudúru* "landmark," *adánu* "season," *sulúmu* "alliance."

It will be seen from this that the accentuation of Assyrian words agrees very remarkably in many particulars with that of Ethiopic as described by Dr. Trumpp in the *Zeitschrift der Deutschen Morgenländischen Gesellschaft*, Vol. xxviii. 4 (1874). See my paper on " The Tenses of the Assyrian Verb," in the *Journal of the Royal Asiatic Society*, Vol. viii., p. 19 (1876).

LECTURE VI.

The Pronoun.

———

THIS evening I come to the pronouns, one of the easiest parts of Assyrian grammar. A definite number of words have to be learned by heart, and there is no need of carrying certain type-forms in the head to be applied to some strange word we may meet in the inscriptions, as is the case with the nouns and verbs. You will observe how closely the Assyrian pronouns resemble those of the other cognate Semitic languages, while some of them present us with older forms which have been lost in the other dialects.

A list of the personal pronouns will be found in my *Elementary Grammar*, p. 57. You will notice that the second syllable of the pronoun of the first person plural is given doubtfully. The word unfortunately is only once found, in the Babylonian text of the famous Behistun inscription (l. 3), and there the reading is uncertain. The first and third characters are clear enough, but the middle one is doubtful. According to Sir H. Rawlinson's cast it looks like ⸤⸥ *ga;* but the analogy of the cognate dialects would lead us to supply some character with the value of *nakh.* You will also notice that both the first and second persons singular have a double form. The first form *anacu* and *atta* or *atti*, is the usual one, and the one, too, which agrees with the ordinary first and second personal pronouns of the other Semitic dialects. *Yāti* and *cātu* have a more substantival force, like our "myself," "thyself," and are accordingly generally found at the beginning of a sentence. Thus we read (*W. A. I.* I., 68; II. 19, 21,) *yāti Nabunahid* "as for me Nabonidus;" *ca-a-tiv a-mat-ka man-nu i-lam-mad* "as for thee, who learns thy will." *Cāta* (the accusative of *cātí*) may, however, be used for the sake of emphasis after a preceding verbal-suffix -*ca* as (Sm. *A*. 183) *usamkhar-ca cāta* "I cause thee, even thee, to be present." It is very interesting as affording us an example of the guttural form of the second personal pronoun used otherwise than as a verbal-suffix, and may be a relic of a very old pronoun which has been lost in the cognate Semitic idioms. The termination both of *cātu* or *cāta* and of *yāti* is the same as that of the feminine in nouns, and of the longer form (*sunutu*, etc.) of the third personal pronoun plural. It will be remembered that the Semitic languages express an abstract idea by a feminine suffix, and in this way we can explain how the feminine termination came to be attached to the personal pronouns when they were employed in an abstract sense ("myself," "thyself," "themselves"). We never meet with the nominative *yātu* or the accusative *yāta* in the case of the first personal pronoun, but only with the lighter case-ending *yāti*. There was something in this latter ending which suited the ears and vocal organs of the Assyrians; *tu* and *ta* had always a tendency to become *ti*, and in some substantives like *tuculti* it is the form almost invariably used. *Yāti* (𒅀𒋾 𒅀 𒋾) was frequently shortened into *yati*, and in one instance (Sm. *A*. 225, 55.) we find *aiti*, according to the Assyrian phonetic law by which *a + a* represents not only *aya* but also *yā* and *ai*. It is interesting that traces of the same pronoun are to be found in the Hebrew '*an-î* for *an-ya*, which denotes the first person as well as the more usual '*anôchi*, and in the Ethiopic *ana* "I," for *an-(y)a*. Besides *yāti*, the longer, more emphatic form *yatima* is met with in the inscriptions, which literally signifies "myself here," *ma* being the suffixed demonstrative pronoun. We shall meet further on with numerous examples of this suffixed pronoun. Instead of *yāti*, however, we sometimes find *ya-a-si* (*yāsi*), which occurs more generally in the middle than at the beginning of a sentence. Thus Sm. *A*. 108, 3, *salim-mu yāsi libba-cunu* "greeting (from) me [as far as I am concerned] to you [your hearts];" 225, 35, *sa naciru sanavva eli yāsi katsu. la ubilu ina libbi* "which no other enemy except me (with) his hand has touched [brought his hand into the midst (of it)]." Elsewhere we have *aisi* just as we have *aiti* by the side of *yāti*. Now although there is no doubt as to the meaning of this word *yāsi* as it is used in the inscriptions, and of its being a synonyme of *yāti*, the origin and real signification of it is extremely hard to settle. Prof. Schrader believes that the termination *si* is a suffix like *ti*; and though he does not go on to say so, I suppose he would connect the suffix with the pronoun *su*, so that *yāsi* (or *yāsu*) would primarily have meant " that me," or " me namely." He has support for this view in the fact that by the side of *sinati* " them," and the suffixed possessive pronoun of the second person plural *cunu* we seem to get also the very rare forms *sinasi* and *cunusi*. Thus in the old Babylonian inscription of Khammuragas at the Louvre, which is one of the oldest inscriptions written in Semitic Assyrian that we possess, and which is certainly earlier than the sixteenth century B.C., we read (ii. 6.) *lu as-cu-un-si-na-si-iv* " I made them," and in Sm. *A.* 108, 4, *lu dhub-cu-nu-si mi-nav-va* " your good deeds are numbered, and." But for my own part I cannot assent to his theory. Considering the similarity that exists between the two characters ⟨⟞ *si* and ⊳⟨⟨ *ti*, and the frequent mistakes committed both by ancient scribes and by modern copyists of the inscriptions, I believe that the two examples quoted above, the only examples, be it remembered, which can be adduced from the whole range of known inscriptions, are simply erroneous readings, and that we ought to read *sinativ* and *cunuti*. Dr. Schrader, it is true, brings forward another instance from the syllabaries (*id-din-su-nu-siv*, etc.') ; but this is a mistake ; the Accadian column shows that the character which he reads *siv* and regards as the suffix of *sunu* is really *sim* " a price " (from שׂום, literally " that which is laid down "). It seems to me, therefore, that *yāsi* or *aisi* stands alone, and is to be explained by the word *aisu* or *y su* (the Heb. אִישׁ) " man " with the suffix of the first personal possessive pronoun " my," so that its original signification will have been " my man," i.e., " myself," like ὅδε ὁ ἀνήρ in Greek.

The second and third personal pronouns are good instances of the use made of the difference in quality between the vowels to express distinction of gender. Both *u* and *a* were liable to be weakened to *i*, and so this vowel was taken to denote the weaker feminine gender when the masculine was represented by *u* or *a*. I have already drawn your attention to the Assyrian tendency to employ *i* in preference to any other vowel after the feminine index *t*. *A* itself was considered more feminine than the labialised *u*, so that when the latter was used in a masculine form *a* was often used in the corresponding feminine. The vowel of the third personal pronoun was properly long, as may be seen by its being frequently written *su-u* and

---

' *W. A. I.* II., 11, 25-28. See Appendix to this Chapter.

sometimes having a double consonant after it when the enclitic *ma* is added (*summa*). It is possible, however, that instead of *summa* or *suma* we ought to read *suva* and *suvva*, and regard the final syllable not as the demonstrative *ma* but as part of the original and fuller form of the third personal pronoun itself. In this case *suva* would exactly represent the Arabic third personal pronoun *hŭwa* "he." Little, constantly-used words like pronouns, however, tend to get rubbed down by friction, and the Assyrian pronouns formed no exception to the rule. *Sū* or *su'u* became *sŭ*, and in certain cases after a preceding *u* it was worn away to a simple *s*. Thus we find *kirbus'* "its interior," instead of *kirbusu, yusadlimus'* "they conferred on him," instead of *yusadlimusu;* and the same contraction takes place in the case of the plural *sunu* and *sina* which become *sun* and *sin*. No precise rules can be laid down as regards this shortening, and euphonic reasons alone seem to have influenced it. Something also, perhaps, depended upon the education of the scribe, as we all know that the language of a lower social grade abounds more in contractions than a literary or court dialect. Purely phonetic reasons, however, must have determined the employment of the longer forms *sunutu*, etc., though desire of emphasis often influenced the choice of them.

Let us now pass on to the pronominal suffixes attached to nouns and verbs.[1] It will be observed that the only difference between the two classes of suffixes exists in the case of the first person singular and the third person plural, which are *ya*, *a* or *i*, and *sunu* and *sina* for nouns, and *anni, áni, inni, ni* and *sunutu* and *sinatu*, as well as *sunu* and *sina*, for verbs. The possessive pronoun of the first person gives us the same root as that which we have met with in the second form of the first personal pronoun (*yáti*), just as the possessive pronoun of the second person gives us the root of the second form of the second personal pronoun. The nasal in the first personal suffix of the verb belongs to the pronoun, but the preceding vowel in *anni* or *áni* (weakened into *inni*) is an union vowel to prevent two consonants from coming together, and the consonant is doubled to show that the accent falls on that union vowel. However, in the Akhæmenian period the union vowel is looked upon as part of the pronoun itself, and the longer form is accordingly used after a vowel-ending, an aspirate being inserted between the two vowels; e.g., *litstsuru-h-anni* "may they protect me," *itticru-h-anni* "they were

[1] A list of these will be found in my *Assyrian Grammar and Reading Book* (Bagster and Sons), pp. 58, 59.

estranged from me." In earlier inscriptions we sometimes find a final *u* coalescing with the initial *a* into *wa*, and as *w* is never written in Assyrian we get forms like *yusatlimanni* for *yusatlimu-anni* "they conferred on me." This *anni* could be weakened to *inni* (i.e., *íni*) and so we meet with *yuraps'-inni* "they enlarged for me." You will notice that the union-vowel *a* could be used with all the pronominal suffixes if the verbal form terminated in a consonant. From my calling it a union-vowel, however, you must not .suppose that I consider it to have been originally one of those convenient figments of old fashioned philology which were imagined to explain every letter otherwise difficult to account for. As a matter of fact, this union-vowel which we have been considering was primarily a tense-termination which we shall have to speak of when we come to the verbs. This tense-termination in -*a* was used when motion was implied and was regularly required, therefore, when the object or accusative followed the verb instead of preceding it. With the second person feminine which ends in -*i* this tense-termination could not be employed, and accordingly the possessive pronominal suffix was attached immediately to the person-ending of the verb, the *n* being doubled to denote that the accent fell upon the preceding syllable (e.g., *tucassipinni* "thou didst reveal to me ").

Just as the pronouns of the third person singular and plural might lose their final vowel, so the possessive pronominal suffix of the second person masculine singular might be reduced to simple *c*, with the accent thrown back upon the syllable which goes before (e.g., *attápsac* for *attappisaca*). On the other hand, if the enclitic conjunction *va* "and" followed, not only was the vowel of the pronoun retained in all its original length, but the *v* was also doubled to show that the accent fell upon the penultima (e.g., *icsudu-sunutav-va.*)

A noun might precede the possessive pronominal suffixes either in the construct state or with the case-endings attached. Thus we may have either *cirib-ca* "the midst of thee," or *cirbi-ca* (for *ciribi-ca*) "thy middle." That is to say, the Assyrian language left it doubtful whether these possessive pronouns were to be treated as substantives or as adjectives. No doubt when they are used with substantives they more commonly have the force of adjectives than of substantives; but when used with verbs they are pure substantives, and the personal pronominal forms *yáti* and *cátu* prove that the substantive suffixes also could be regarded as substantival. In the case of the first person pronominal suffix there is one form which is always treated as a substantive. This is *i* which is suffixed only to the construct state of the noun, as *ab-i* "my father" ("father of me"), *bint-i* "my daughter" ("daughter of me"). In Babylonian inscriptions the form in *a* could be used in the same way, and we could have *ab-a* and *bint-a*, just as in the Assyrian dialect we have *ab-i* and *bint-i*. In Assyrian, however, the form in *a* could only be used adjectively, e.g., *abu-a* "my father." Instead of *a*, *ya* was more generally employed, partly to avoid the hiatus of two vowels coming together, partly because *ya* was the more primitive form of the word. After a long *ā*, *ya* became *ai* according to a common phonetic law of Assyrian which I have noticed before. Thus "my knees" is *bircā-ai* instead of *bircā-ya*, "my feet" *ṣepā-ai* instead of *ṣepā-ya*, where the nouns are in the dual number.·

A phonetic change occasioned by the attachment of the third personal possessive pronoun to a substantive may puzzle a beginner very much. We often come across forms like *khirisu*, *bisu*, *rupusu*. How are these to be explained? By the action of two rules, one relating to the writing and the other to the phonology of the language. You will remember that a double letter is very frequently left unexpressed in writing, and so such forms as those just quoted stand for *khirissu*, *bissu*, *rupussu*. These again are for *khirit-su*, *bit-su*, *ruput-su*, *t* being assimilated to the following sibilant; while the sibilant *š* itself is a modification of *s*, *s* being changed into *š* after a dental according to a phonetic law of Assyrian to which I drew your attention in an earlier lecture. *Khirisu*, therefore, is nothing more than *khirit-su* "its ditch," *bisu*, *bit-su* "his house," *rupusu*, *ruput-su* "his greatness."

The only other point I need notice in relation to these pronouns is the appearance of an intensified form of the possessive pronoun by means of the substantive *'attū*, in the later period of the language. In Assur-bani-pal's inscriptions we read *sa la iptallakhu abi-ya va attū-a* "who revere not my fathers and me," where the word *attū*, is used in exactly the same way as the corresponding Heb. אוֹת or אֵת to mark the accusative. The word signifies "existence," and may possibly be connected with the analogous Arabic *'iyyā*. It was only when the language had, as it were, grown old, and the true and original force and meaning of the case-endings had tended to be forgotten altogether that any necessity arose for a new method of denoting the accusative case. Just as in Hebrew, which it must be remembered is linguistically a later form of Semitic speech than Assyrian, so in Assyrian the same machinery came to be used to mark the objective case of the pronoun. No doubt in popular conversation this machinery had long been employed, but we do not find it in the literary language of the inscriptions till the closing days of the Empire. In the disintegration afterwards undergone by the language, when it had come into contact with foreign influences and become affected by an Aramaising tendency, the construction of the possessive pronoun with 'attū underwent a great development, and the inscriptions of the Akhæmenian period are filled with instances of it. Where the classical language would have been contented with simply saying *zir-ya* " my race," the Akhæmenian language has *zir-ya attū-a* (literally " my race (which is) to me "), or *attū-a abū-a* " my own father," instead of the simple *abū-a*. This extended use of *attū* with the pronominal suffixes is one of the characteristics of the Akhæmenian stage of Assyrian.

The next pronouns to be considered are the demonstratives. Here, again, the lists given in the Grammar must be committed to memory, with the exception of the forms enclosed within brackets, which are filled in from analogy and do not occur in the inscriptions.

Su'atu and *sāsu* are employed indifferently, but *sāsu* may be used alone in place of the separate personal pronouns. *Su'atu* is merely a secondary form of the third personal pronoun *su'u* (Hebrew הוא) with the termination *tu* attached, which has here lost entirely its feminine signification. Just as *si*, therefore, is a weakened form of the feminine *sa*, *si'atu* makes its appearance by the side of *sātu* or *sa'atu*.

Aga or *hagā* is a product of the Akhæmenian period which is not found in any earlier inscriptions. The fluctuating form of the common gender singular and plural, as well as the absence of any distinguishing mark of either gender or number, the termination of the feminine singular having been apparently an after-thought, seem to imply that the word was a borrowed one, and this view is strengthened by the fact that it is not found until the time when the language had been subjected to foreign contact and influences. Dr. Schrader asserts that the pronoun has an undoubtedly Semitic look, and in my *Assyrian Grammar* I have with considerable hesitation been inclined to take the same view; but I now think that Sir Henry Rawlinson and M. Oppert are rather in the right when they refer the origin of the word to some Turanian source. It may be Parthian, or it may be Susianian. It is frequently employed like a mere article, another instance of the subjection of the Assyrian, which had no article, to foreign influences and of the late linguistic character of the Akhæmenian dialect. Thus we find *aga sadu* "this mountain," *agannitu matâti* "these countries." Its use as an article, however, was not yet fixed, and it might follow as well as precede its noun, as in *matâti agannet, sarrutu agata*, "this sovereignty," *same agata* "this heaven," *irtsitiv agata* "this earth." It will be observed that it is the inflected form of the pronoun which generally follows the noun; and this inflected feminine form was given to it after its adoption into the Assyrian language and in accordance with the analogy of other adjectives and pronouns. This is shown by the fact that *aga* is still used without any inflection at all for both masculine and feminine, singular and plural. From its employment as a quasi-article, *agā* came to be compounded with the pronouns *annu* and *su* which it served to intensify; and hence we get singular *agannu* and *aganna*, and plural masculine *agannutu*, feminine *agannitu* or *aganet*, as well as *aga-su* and *aga-sunu*.

Determinative distance was expressed in Assyrian (as in Latin or Greek) by three demonstratives, *ammu* or *mā*, being *hic*, ὅδε, "he here by me," *annu*, *iste*, οὗτος, "he by you," and *ullu*, *ille*, ἐκεῖνος, "he there by him." *Ammu* never occurs; but the feminine singular *ammāte* does, and this is sufficient to support the correctness of the conjectural form. *Ammu* seems to have been driven out of use by *su'atu* and *sāsu*, and instead of it we have the contracted form of the accusative singular *mā*, which was still further shortened into *mă* (like *sŭ* from *sū*) and then attached to nouns and pronouns as an enclitic. *Mā* came also to be used for the masculine plural, and so we read (Sm. *A.* 156, 50) *mā sa icbudu* "those who laboured." I have already spoken of the attachment of this enclitic demonstrative to the pronoun *yāti*, producing *yātima*; but one of its most frequent uses is with the pronoun *annu* as in *ultu usmani annite-ma* "from that camp here," *anni-ma* or *an-ma* "this person here," i.e., "myself." *Su'atu* may even be added after it for the sake of emphasis, as in the phrase *ina sanati-ma siati* "in this very year." The enclitic demonstrative serves to refer the attention to something which has been mentioned before, and so answers to our "said" or "aforesaid," as in *sar Assur-ma* "king of the said Assyria," and from this sense it passes into that of "accordingly," "also," "in the same place," or "at the same time." This use of *ma* is especially common in the astrological tablets.[1] The explanation of *ma* and its connection with *ammāte* were first pointed out by Mr. Norris. Prof. Schrader holds a different view, reading *va* instead of *ma* and regarding it as a sort of waw consecutive, i.e., an enclitic "and," added in places where it would be impossible to translate it, as two co-ordinate sentences are not joined together. Parallel passages are adduced from the Old Testament to show that a similar construction may be found in Hebrew, and certainly so far as the historical inscriptions go Prof. Schrader's very plausible and tempting theory might be maintained. But the astrological tablets absolutely forbid it and prevent our regarding the word as anything else than a pronoun. However, I hope to return to this point and discuss it more fully in a future lecture.

About *annu* and *ullu* there can be no dispute as to either their origin or their nature. They are pronouns which are to be found in the other Semitic dialects and are of very frequent use. Another form of *annu* is 𒀭 ➤𒁹 ⊬ (Sm. *A.* 103, *W. A. I.* II., 60, 11.), in which the initial character seems to stand for *h* and to show that '*annu* was properly pronounced *hannu*. *Ullu* is used absolutely

---

[1] Thus one of these tablets (*W. A. I.*, 58, No. 7,) concludes as follows :

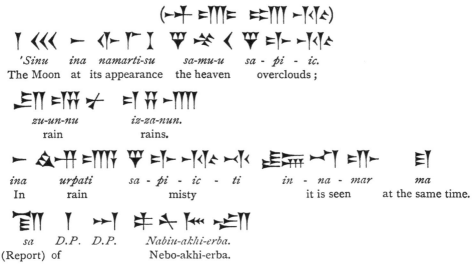

'*Sinu*	*ina*	*namarti-su*	*sa-mu-u*	*sa - pi - ic.*	
The Moon	at	its appearance	the heaven	overclouds ;	

zu-un-nu	*iz-za-nun.*
rain	rains.

ina	*urpati*	*sa - pi - ic - ti*	*in - na - mar*	*ma*
In	rain	misty	it is seen	at the same time.

sa	D.P.	D.P.	*Nabiu-akhi-erba.*
(Report) of			Nebo-akhi-erba.

in the common phrase *ultu ullu* "from that (time)," meaning "from old time," or "long since," (like the Hebrew מֵאָז). In the Akhæmenian period, an adjective *ulluai* "on the further side," makes its appearance, derived from *ullu*, and formed like gentilic adjectives in -*ai*, such as *tihamtai* "the seaman," *Parsai* "a Persian," *Babilai* "a Babylonian," so that the word literally means "the one over there." *Ullī* with long *i* also occurs as a masculine plural instead of the more regular *ullutu*, and formed after the analogy of masculine plural nouns or the common gender plural of *annu*. One of the inscriptions of Xerxes presents us with the strange compound *akhullai ulli* which has to be decomposed into *akhi* "shores," *ullai* "over there," and *ullī* "those." This is a specimen of the way in which classical Assyrian had become corrupted in the Akhæmenian age, and affords a reason for the inadvisability of the student's beginning with this form of the language, although he would thus be following out the historical course of the decipherment, which began with the trilingual inscriptions.

The relative pronoun *sa* must now be considered, more especially since comparative researches have shown that both in Semitic and Aryan, as well as in other classes of languages, the relative was primarily a demonstrative. Accordingly this relative pronoun *sa* has the same origin as the demonstrative *sāsu* and the third personal pronoun *su*; and it is found in Phœnician inscriptions, in the northern and later Hebrew of the Song of Solomon and the books of Judges and Ecclesiastes, and in Rabbinic Hebrew. You will find traces of it also in some of the proper names of the Old Testament; among the antediluvian patriarchs, for instance, *Methu-sa-el*, is a purely Assyrian formation which would appear in the inscriptions as *mutu-sa-ili* "man of God." I may observe by the way, that many of the obscure names that occur in the early chapters of Genesis are likely to receive their explanation from the Assyrian monuments; thus Abel, as M. Oppert long ago pointed out, is the Assyrian *'abilu* "a son," and Noah seems to be referable to the same root as *Anu*. To turn now from the question of derivation to that of use, the relative is very extensively employed in Assyrian in all sorts of senses. One of these is illustrated by the compound *Methu-sa-el*, where *sa* preceded by the nominative case of the noun replaces the construct state and expresses what is called the periphrastic genitive. Just as the modern languages of Europe have passed into an analytic stage, substituting analytical constructions for inflection, so in Assyrian the peri-phrastic genitive came more and more, with the lapse of centuries, to replace the older construct state. Instead of *sar Assuri*, therefore, we get *sarru sa Assuri*, literally "the king which (is) Assur," and so "king of Assur." Hence *sa* may very often be translated by our preposition "of." The second noun properly retains the genitive ending, although in the general decay of the case-system in Assyrian other case-endings came in time to be used. In the common language of every day life, the first noun might even be omitted altogether in certain well-known phrases, as for instance in the contract tablets where we frequently read *ina sa Gargamis* "according to (the maneh) of Carchemish," with *mana* understood. As in the case of our "that," *sa* is sometimes to be rendered by the conjunction "that;" frequently also we can translate it only by "where" or "when," in passages where the word properly means "(at) which (place)," or "(at) which (time)." *Sa* may be pleonastically employed at the beginning of a sentence to refer to the whole passage that has gone before, where we must render it "as regards which." Thus we have *sa ana natsir citte va misari-su* "as regards which (city) for the protection of its ordinances and laws;" and when a word which ought to be in the genitive is placed at the commencement of a sentence owing to its being first and most prominent in the thought of the speaker (like "*moi*," or "*La chose où est-elle*" in French), *sa* in the sense of "as regards," is put before it, in order to avoid its being used absolutely and without construction. So in a curious catalogue of the astronomical works contained in the Library of Sargon at Agané, now nearly four thousand years old, we read *sa sanati arkhi-sa sa arkhi yumi-su(nu)* "of (as regards) the year its months, of (as regards) the months their days," where you will observe the insertion of the possessive pronominal suffixes *sa* and *sunu*. In fact the relative almost always requires the noun following as well as the verb to have a pronominal suffix attached, as *Yahudu sa asar-su ru'ku* "Judah whose situation (is) remote," (literally "of which its place"), *sa ina 'abli-su* "on whose son." Of course, to the mind of the Assyrian, *sa* always had the relative force "who" or "which," however much the idiom of our own language may require us to translate it sometimes by "of," sometimes by "when" or "where." Just as in English and Hebrew, so in Assyrian the relative could be omitted altogether, especially in poetry; e.g., *bilata va mandatta issa'a* "the tribute and gifts (which) he brought;" *itti kari ab-i iczuru* "with the forts my father had made." I need not add that *sa* is indeclinable, and accordingly takes the same form with final *a* as *ma* when that first demonstrative pronoun is used indeclinably.

Of the interrogative pronoun *mannu* there is nothing to be said except that it enters into the composition of the indefinite pronouns, and in the later Akhæmenian period of the language is itself used indefinitely, as at Behistun where we have *mannu atta sarru* "whatever king thou (mayest be)." The indefinite pronoun may be omitted in a subordinate clause, as in *ikhkhira abdhu amattu sa pī-su ustenna* "(whoever) evades a pledge, the truth of his mouth changes." A very common indefinite pronoun is the indeclinable *mala* or *mal* "as many as," especially frequent in the phrase *mala basu* or *mal basu* "as many as exist." Prof. Schrader is doubtless right in deriving it from the root מלא "to fill," so that its original meaning was "fulness," like *meluv* "a flood," from the same root. He compares the use of the Hebrew מְלֹא in passages like Ex. ix. 8. The "fulness" of a thing is the whole of it, as much as there is in it; and so *mala* came to have its pronominal signification. It is a good example of a presentative word becoming a representative one, of a substantive passing into a pronoun, a process which is still going on in our own language. Now and then the inscriptions afford us instances of the employment of *mala* in its primary sense. Thus Assur-bani-pal says of himself *anacu Assur-bani-pal sar mat Assuri sa ina ci-bit ili rabuti im-tsu-u ma-la lib-bi-su* "I am Assur-bani-pal who by the command of the great gods the fulness of his heart (i.e., all that is in his heart) has found."

The reflexive pronoun *rāmanu* "self," was first explained by M. Oppert. It is an instance of the phonetic law in Assyrian by which a *kh* may become simple *h*. *Rāmanu*, therefore, stands for *rahmanu*, and this for *rakhmanu*, a lengthened form of the Hebrew רֶחֶם "bowels," from which we have also the Assyrian *rihma* "mercy," and *rahimu* "loving." According to Harkavy the latter word *rahimu* explains the second part of the proper name Abraham (not Abram), which would then signify "the loving father," a fitting title for "the friend of God." Now this *rahmanu* "the bowels" or "innermost parts of one," came easily to denote "oneself," just as in the other Semitic languages the conception of "oneself" is derived metaphorically from words which denote parts of the body, more especially the inward parts. Thus in Hebrew, Arabic and Aramaic *nephesh* " life " or " soul," the Assyrian *napistu*, came to signify " oneself," and even in Assyrian we meet with this metaphorical use of the word in a passage where Assur-bani-pal says *napista-su ikdhil* " he slew his life," i.e., " himself " (Sm. *A.* 104, 56). So in Hebrew *etsem* " bone," Assyrian *atsmu*, acquired the same reflexive signification as in the well-known expression " bone of my bone," and *res* or " head," Assyrian *risu*, in Ethiopic. Another word which passed in Assyrian from a concrete to a reflexive meaning was *gadu* " a piece cut off,". (Hebrew גֵּדֶע) and so " an individual," e.g., *su-su-bu šar Babili ga-du cim-ti-su pal-dhu-šu-un ci-rib mat-ya u-bil-su* " Susub king of Babylon, himself, (and) his family, alive, within my country I brought." *Gadu* may be combined with *sāsu;* thus *sāsu gadu;* and *sāsu* itself is occasionally found in a reflexive sense. I have already mentioned that *annima* or *anma* signifies " myself."

I must not dismiss the pronouns without noticing the little word *cala* or *cal* " all," which like *mala* is used with a plural verb. Unlike *mala*, however, *cal* had a secondary form which admitted of the feminine *cullatu.* Both *cal* and *cala* were used with the genitive, the final *a* of *cala* being apparently regarded as a radical and therefore already in the construct state. Thus we meet with *cala simi u etsi* " all plants and trees," as well as *cal musi* " all night." *Calama* " the world," and hence " all sorts," has nothing to do with this *cala* as Prof. Schrader supposed, but is an Accadian word which was borrowed by the Assyrians. An example of its use in the Assyrian inscriptions occurs in Bellino's Cylinder, iv. 20: *Sin-akhi-erba a-sa-rid-dan mal-ci mu-di-e sip-ri ca-la-ma* " Sennacherib, the first born of kings, knowing the interpretation of all things," (or " the languages of the world ").

APPENDIX TO LECTURE VI.

See page 65.

I have left my objections to Dr. Schrader's view in the text, though I am now less disinclined to accept it than I was. Certainly in *W. A. I.* II., 11, 27 and 28, we find *si* and not *sim*, the whole passage reading thus :—

ACCADIAN.		ASSYRIAN.	
[*in-nan-*] *sin-sum*		*id-din-su-nu-sim*	" he gave them."
[*in-nan-*] *sin-summus*		*id-di-nu-su-nu-sim*	" they gave them."
[*in-nan-*] *sin-summu*		*i-na-din-su-nu-si*	" he gives them."
[*in-nan-*] *sin-summune*		*i-na-di-nu-su-nu-si*	" they give them."

If Dr. Delitzsch is right (Smith's *Chaldäische Genesis*, p. 320), the verbal form *icarrabannasi* which occurs in the 26th line of the 4th column of the Deluge tablets is to be explained " he brings near to us," *annasi* being the suffixed first person possessive pronoun, with the termination *si*.

LECTURE VII.

The Verb.

W E have now travelled through what may be called the first part of the Assyrian grammar, and have reached the verbs, here as in all languages the most difficult and intricate but at the same time the most necessary part of the whole subject. As in the other Semitic idioms the Assyrian verb is for the most part triliteral, that is to say, its root, when denuded of all flexions, consists of three radical consonants accompanied by vowels which differ in different forms. The triliteral nature of the verb is a great help to us in our decipherment of the inscriptions; not only does it enable us to decide what values are to be assigned to the characters (as was remarked in a former lecture), but it also lets us see at a glance what parts of the word are formative and what radical, i.e., what the root of it must be. Attempts have frequently been made to resolve all the triliteral Semitic verbs into biliteral monosyllables by scholars who have been trained in Aryan philology, and so imbued with the idea that the roots of all classes of languages must be monosyllabic; but such attempts make havoc with Semitic philology and are decidedly opposed to the testimony of the Assyrian monuments, where verbs which in the other idioms now consist of two consonants only and a vowel are still represented by three consonants. In fact four of the letters of the Semitic alphabet, *h*, *v*, *y*, and *e*, are semi-vowels (or more properly semi-consonants), and may therefore easily pass into vowels with the course of centuries and the carelessness of ordinary pronunciation. Comparative philology teaches us that one of the great causes of change in language is phonetic decay, and in accordance with this principle, while consonants

become vocalised (as in French *haut* fr. *altus*, or our own common pronunciation of *walk* and *talk*,) vowels do not conversely become consonants. In
strict harmony with this we find the original semi-consonants in Assyrian
verbs, where in Hebrew and the other Semitic tongues these have been
reduced to mere vowels. Thus where Hebrew gives us כָּוָה and לָוָה (written
you will observe כוה and לוה, but preserving the final aspirate, which has
been lost in Assyrian, at all events in writing), Assyrian has *alvi'* " I cling
to," and *acvi'* (or possibly *acmi*) " I burned." In the grammars and vocabularies drawn up by the scribes of Assur-bani-pal, the oldest grammars, by
the way, of which we know, the so-called biliteral roots are carefully assigned
three radicals, showing that Semitic triliteration is not an invention of modern
grammarians but a fact recognised instinctively by the earliest speakers of
a Semitic language who attempted to systematise its forms.

Originally, therefore, we may assume that every *true* Semitic root,
borrowed ones being excluded, consisted of three consonants ; but that in
course of time these consonants were worn away by phonetic decay, and
in many cases became transformed into vowels. Hence have arisen the
defective or *weak* verbs, which contain one or more of these semi-consonantal
radicals, and so appear in all or many of their forms with less than the
prescribed number of three consonant radicals. Take, for instance, the root
which means " to come." This is written בוא in Hebrew, where the final
aleph preserves the memory of the final aspirate which originally ended the
word. The medial radical, however, has become the vowel *u*. Now turn to
Assyrian. Here the final aspirate has been lost altogether, at least so far
as the writing is concerned, and the only traces of it which can be found
are where the verbal form has a vowel ending suffixed to a flexion which ends
in a vowel (e.g., *issa'a* for *issā* " he raised," from נשא). But, on the other
hand, the medial consonant which has disappeared in Hebrew remains in
many forms in Assyrian, and so we still meet with the infinitive or verbal
noun *bavu* instead of *bu*. *Bavu*, however, on account of its frequent use, has
not preserved its medial consonant in Assyrian so well as the majority of
other roots with medial *v*, and hence we get *ibu* " they came " instead of *ibvu*,
and *bu* " they are coming," instead of *bavu*. So, too, in the derivatives we
have *butu* " a coming," instead of *bavutu*, a word very often used in the
construct case after *ina* in the sense of " over against," as *ina bu-ut babi*

rabi-su "over against his great gate," as well as *tibu* (construct case, *tib*) "an onset," formed with the prefix *t*, where every letter of the root has been lost except the first. But the Assyrian language not only preserves the *v* sound where in Hebrew it has passed into a vowel, but it gives us some reason for believing that even this semi-vowel or semi-consonant itself is an instance of phonetic decay, and that *v*, in many cases at all events, implies a preceding full consonant. You will remember the interchange that there is in the writing between *m* and *v*, the same character standing for both sounds, and the grounds there are for holding that this interchange was not peculiar to the Accadian alone and found in the Assyrian inscriptions only from their making use of the Accadian syllabary, but that it existed at some time or other in the Assyrian language itself. Now if we take this very root *bavu* "to come," and suppose the *v* to have come from an earlier *m*, we obtain *bamu*, from which we could easily form the feminine noun *bamatu*, for which the Hebrew would give us בָּמָה. Now what do we find in both Assyrian and Hebrew? This very word *bamatu* or בָּמָה meaning "a high place," and hence "an altar." But is not a high place that which one "comes" up to? and so are we not justified in thinking that this word *bamatu* was derived from the root בוא before the medial *m* had been changed first into *v* and then into *u*, though after the loss of the final radical? If this etymology can be supported, high places for the sake of worship would have been known to and named by the Semites at a very early period of their history.

This digression has drawn us away from the Assyrian verb, to which we must return. Just as the verbs which do not contain three full consonant radicals are termed *weak* or *defective*, so those which have their proper complement are termed *strong* or *full*. In speaking of the verb, I shall deal first of all with the strong verb, and then, when this has been thoroughly mastered, pass on to the weak verb. The forms of the one will be the forms of the other, except in so far as they are modified by the loss of letters and the consequent coalescing of vowels. After this I shall say a few words about verbs which contain more than three radicals, most of which are quadriliterals. There are very few of them in Assyrian, and they may be explained partly by the composition of two roots which are run one into the other, partly by the insertion of *r* or *l* in a root, proceeding from the action of a principle directly contrary to that of phonetic decay, which I have named the principle of Emphasis in my book on Comparative Philology.

Dr. Hincks once called Assyrian the Sanskrit of the Semitic idioms, and so far as the artificial regularity of the verbal conjugation is concerned there is a strong likeness between the two languages. Like Hebrew, Assyrian starts with four primary conjugations, the first of which gives us the simple verb with its various inflexions of mood and tense, and may be compared with the active voice of a Latin verb. In accordance with ordinary nomenclature of Semitic grammar we term it the Kal conjugation. To this Kal conjugation answers a passive conjugation called Niphal, characterised by the prefix *n*, so that if we take *iscun* " he made," the third person singular aorist indicative as the type of Kal, *issacin* (for *insacin*) " he is made " will be the type of Niphal. We must be careful, however, about confusing Aryan and Semitic notions of grammar. As we shall see, the tenses of the Semitic verb are not tenses in our sense of the word, i.e., they do not imply any idea of time; and in the same way the passive voice Niphal is not exactly passive in the way that *amari* is the passive of *amare*. Generally speaking Niphal must be translated by a passive, and where Kal is active Niphal is always passive, but there are instances in which it would be a mistake to render Niphal by the passive voice. However, though we cannot exactly call Niphal a passive *voice*, we may call it a passive *conjugation*, and as such it stands to Kal in the relation of passive to active. Next to Niphal comes an *intensive* conjugation which we term Pael, formed by doubling the second radical and (in Assyrian) by combining the vowel *u* with all the person-prefixes. *Yusaccin* " he did make," is a type of this conjugation, where you will observe that the vowel *u* coalesces with the prefix of the third person singular. This vowel *u* is of importance, because owing to the frequent habit the Assyrian scribes had of not expressing a reduplicated consonant in writing, the reduplication of the second radical is often omitted in the inscriptions, and our only means of knowing whether a verbal form belongs to the Pael conjugation or not, is by seeing whether or not it had the performative *u*. I think we may trace in the doubling of the radical the intensive idea expressed by Pael. The machinery of Semitic grammar is for the most part very simple, and depends more on inner change in the vowels and consonants of the root than on external accretion as in our own group of languages. Hence it preserved into civilised times one of the oldest contrivances of speech for marking emphasis and intensity. From its intensive signification Pael sometimes comes to have a causative force; thus *ina zi-ki-ip u-za-kip* "on stakes I impaled;" and when Kal is intransitive Pael is transitive, the Kal *icsud*, for instance, is "he approached," but the Pael *yucassid* "he made to approach."

The last of the primary conjugations is a causative one, termed Shaphel, and distinguished by an initial *s* and (as in Pael) a preformative *ŭ*. Thus *yusascin* is "he caused to make." *S*, at all events initial *s*, tended to become the aspirate *h* in the Semitic tongues, and so, just as the Assyrian third personal pronoun *su* is הוא in Hebrew, the Assyrian Shaphel with *s* is represented by the Hebrew Hiphil with *h*. In all languages an aspirate, particularly at the beginning of a word, is likely to be dropped, and hence it is that in Assyrian we meet with a conjugation Aphel by the side of Shaphel, in which the *s* has been lost altogether after first becoming *h*. Aphel is only found in a special class of defective verbs, those, namely, the middle radical of which is a semi-consonant passing into a vowel. Thus from *dhavabu* "to be good," we get *yudhib* "he was good," instead of *yusadhib*. Aphel, therefore, must be treated as another form of Shaphel and as constituting but a single conjugation with it.

To each of these four primary conjugations the Assyrians regularly assigned two secondary ones, one characterised by the dental *t*, the other by the syllable *tan*. These secondary conjugations had a reflexive force, which, however, frequently became simply intensive, and in the case of Istaphal from Shaphel desiderative. The dental was always inserted into the root immediately after the first radical, except in the case of concave verbs where it often stands before the first radical. Thus from *iscun* we should have *istacun*, but from *dhavabu*, *itdhib*. The longer form in *tan* may possibly be due to Accadian influence, as causatives are formed in that language by means of the word *tan*.[1] By the help of these secondary conjugations the four primary conjugations are tripled in number, and so we have an Iphteal and Iphtaneal by the side of Kal, an Ittaphal and Ittanaphal by the side of Niphal, an Iphtaal and Iphtanaal by the side of Niphal, and an Istaphal and Istanaphal by the side of Shaphel, while Aphel also had its Itaphal and possibly its Itanaphal. But these were not all the secondary conjugations admitted by the Assyrian

[1] Also *ta*, *dan*, and *da*.

verb. The systematising character of the Assyrian literary language regarded Pael as an intensified form of Kal just as Niphal was its passive form, and accordingly required the other two primary conjugations Niphal and Shaphel to be provided with an intensive form corresponding to Pael the intensive form of Kal. Hence arose the two conjugations Niphael and Shaphael, which are, however, chiefly confined to those defective verbs which terminate with a semi-consonant. Examples of them are *illakki* "it was taken," and *yusnammir* "he caused to shine."

Even now, however, we have not ended our list of the Assyrian conjugations. Iphteal, Pael, Shaphel, Aphel, and Istaphal, all had forms containing the vowel *u*, which we may call passive after the fashion of Arabic grammarians. But it must be remembered that they have little in their meaning which we connect with the idea of the passive voice. Examples of these passives are *yunummir* (the passive of Pael) "it was seen," *yussupula* (for *yusasupula*) "he was caused to be overthrown," *yudhbu* "they were made good."

Besides these passives each conjugation, the aorist of Kal excepted, possessed a bye-form in which the vowel which followed or preceded the first radical was *e* or *i*. Thus in Shalmaneser's inscription (*W. A. I.*, 8, l. 100) we have *i-me-ez-zir* (present Kal), and elsewhere we find the Niphals *in-nim-me-du* and *in-ni-ri-su*, the Paels *yunecim, yusepic* and *yunecis*, the Shaphels *yusescin* and *yusecnis*, the Istaphal *ultesib* and the Iphteals and Iphtaals *iptekid* and *yuptekid*. In these cases the second vowel has been affected by that of the final syllable. Among the quadriliteral verbs an instance of this change is met with in *ippisiddu ;* and concave and לי״ה verbs present us with forms like *iserri* "he works," *iritti* "he arranges," *itellu* "they imprison," *ikhissu* "they shook," *isissi* "he says," where the double consonant denotes the length of the preceding vowel. As regards the concave verbs, the forms just quoted are aorists and really quite regular ; the other forms, however, from verbs לי״ה are presents, and must be explained by the fact that the final radical is ע (*isissi* being the Hebrew שׁסע "to persuade;" *iserri*, Hebrew שׁרע "to stretch," etc.) and that this modifies the preceding tense-vowel.

One or two other verbal forms occur in the inscriptions, which we must refer to conjugations sporadically met with in the cognate Semitic idioms. The only one of these that need be mentioned is a Palel, which repeats the last radical and regularly occurs in defective verbs whose medial consonant is a semi-vowel. In these verbs Palel has a preformative *u*, as in *yucnin* "he established," but in some other instances of the conjugation (e.g., *acsuttu* "I acquired,") this preformative is not found. However, it is often very difficult to say whether the doubling of the last radical of a verb, where no vowel intervenes, is an instance of Palel or an irregular mode of showing that the last syllable but one is accented, and some of the examples given in my *Assyrian Grammar* may really be due to the latter cause alone. But in a form like *iddanan* "he gives," (for *indanan*) such a doubt is removed.

Every conjugation possesses certain moods and tenses. It will be convenient to take the tenses first, always remembering that a Semitic tense is by no means the same as a tense in one of our own group of languages. There is no idea of time at the bottom of it, only of relation. Thus it does not express *when* a thing was done, but simply the relation in which the doing of a thing stands to us, i.e., whether it has only just been begun, or whether it is in the course of being done, or whether it is completed. Thus in Latin *amat* means "he loves," namely at the present moment, *amavit* "he loved," at some preceding period, and *amabit* "he will love," in the future; but in Semitic we can only speak of loving being complete or incomplete, definite or indefinite, without any reference whatever to the time at which the act takes place. Hence the Semitic verb possessed originally but one tense which merely denoted action without implying time at all. In the course of centuries, however, another tense grew up, formed by attaching the personal pronouns to the participle present or *nomen agentis*, and therefore signifying "loving-I," that is a permanent or complete state of loving. These personal pronouns were at the outset attached to nouns of all kinds besides the present participle, and only became confined to the latter in Assyrian as the language developed; and the Assyrian has thrown a flood of light upon this part of Semitic philology by preserving traces of this early stage of tense-formation down into historical times. Along with the tense which Dr. Hincks called permansive, and which is called the perfect in the Grammars of other Semitic idioms, we find examples in the inscriptions of formations created in exactly the same manner as the permansive or perfect, except that the personal pronouns are attached not to the participle present but to other nouns as well. Thus besides *dabsacu* "I mature," (formed by attaching *acu*, shortened from *anacu*, to the participle *dabis*,) we have the intransitives *ŝarracu* " I am king," from *ŝarru*, and *asariddacu* " I am chief," from *asaridu*.   In the cognate dialects these older formations are entirely or almost entirely lost, and though philology had already guessed at the origin of the Semitic perfect, had it not been for the decipherment of Assyrian the guess would never have been raised to a certainty.   We now know, however, how the perfect or permansive, the second of the two primary tenses of the Semitic verb, came into existence, and we also know that it did so in comparatively historical times.   As soon as the new tense became fixed, the vagueness of the single primitive tense was limited, and the new tenses were set one against the other as implying the completeness or incompleteness, the definiteness or indefiniteness of an action.   Hence the perfect or permansive came to signify that an action is permanent either in its progress or in its results, while the other tense, called the imperfect in other Semitic Grammars, but which for reasons presently to be given must be termed the aorist in Assyrian, meant that an action was incomplete or took place only at some particular moment. Instead of being extended over a long space of time it occured either at some single definite moment or during a series of isolated moments.   Thus " I know " would be in the perfect or permansive, but " I knew at some particular time " would be in the aorist.   The perfect confines our attention to a definite period and a definite action, but both are left indefinite by the aorist as being able to happen at any moment.

Now most of the Semitic languages were contented with these two tenses only.   Assyrian, however, like Æthiopic, came under the influence of a foreign non-Semitic language which possessed tenses with temporal signification. The Assyrian had received his arts, his science, his theology, and his culture, from the agglutinative Accadian ; his literature was founded on the libraries of the latter ; and he grew up under the cramping influences of this dead language like the literary classes of mediæval Europe under the shadow of Latin.   His mode of thought came to be moulded by that of the Accadian, and so, just as the Frankish conquerors of Gaul infused into the dialect of the provincials Teutonic idioms like *avaler* (*ad vallem*) for *zu Thal gehen* or *contrée* (*contrata* [*terra*]) for *Gegend* (*gegen*), the distinctions of Accadian grammar came to be introduced into Assyrian.   The existing machinery was adapted to new purposes, and forms which once had the same meaning were now differentiated and appropriated to the expression of different and definite senses. No doubt the dialect of the uneducated long resisted this differentiating tendency, and in this way we can explain how it is that the signification assigned to a particular form in the majority of instances is not always to be observed in it, but that exceptions exist in the use of the several verbal forms. We must also bear in mind that with the growth of civilisation would naturally arise a need of more explicitly and clearly marking out the elements of time in a sentence than was originally the case, and that the verb would therefore become more developed and express more and more what we mean by tenses. We can trace the effects of this tendency in Hebrew and Arabic where a foreign influence like that of Accadian upon Assyrian has been absent. The development of temporal signification in the verb was brought out in the case of Hebrew by means of position, a pluperfect force, for instance, being given by placing the subject between the copula and the perfect, in the case of Arabic by particles like *kad*. Neither of these languages, however, could attain to that clearness of temporal signification in the verb which the Assyrian was able to reach by the help of Accadian. It is important to bear this in mind, because in spite of my explanations and the notorious example of Æthiopic, I have been misunderstood in what I have said upon this point and have been imagined to state that Assyrian independently and without assistance obtained a glimpse of that conception of the verb which lies at the bottom of all our Aryan tongues.

After having said so much by way of preface I must now point out what was the extent of temporal signification ever attained by the Assyrian verb, and what were the means employed for giving it this signification. To repeat what has already been said, Assyrian possessed two primary tenses in common with the other Semitic languages, one of them answering to the perfect, the other to the imperfect of Hebrew or Arabic or Aramaic. The imperfect was originally the sole tense of the Semitic verb, but before the separation of the several dialects the perfect also had begun to be formed and contrasted with the imperfect. The perfect we have named the permansive in Assyrian following Dr. Hincks's nomenclature and for want of a better designation; the imperfect divided itself in Assyrian into a variety of different forms. In speaking of the conjugations I have quoted the third person singular of what I have termed the aorist, the type-form of which in Kal, you will remember, is *iscun*. Now *iscun* contains the root *s-c-n* with the personal prefix *i*, and but a single connecting vowel between the second and third radical. This is the form most common in the inscriptions; in an ordinary historical inscription, for instance, seventy per cent of the verbal forms will be those in which the last radical of the third person singular closes a syllable. They answer to the apocopated imperfects in Arabic and to the ordinary form of the imperfect in Hebrew. But though this form is by far the most usual one in the inscriptions which we have to decipher, it was by no means the original form of the imperfect of the Semitic verb. It was at a comparatively late period that the last radical came to close a syllable; primarily the last radical was always followed by a vowel. In fact, the original Semitic tense was treated just like a noun and considered to differ from any other noun only in implying a particular kind of relation, like the Greek infinitive with the article prefixed or the infinitive and gerunds in Latin. Hence, just as the Semitic noun terminated in *-u*, *-i* and *-a*, or with the mimmation in *-um*, *-im*, and *-am*, so the verbal tense also terminated in the same way. The ending in *-a* or *-am* which marks the accusative in the noun, that is to say the point to which the mind travels, denotes motion to a point or rest in a point in the verb, and hence would be employed (1) where the object or accusative immediately follows the verb, (2) where the sentence is conditional, i.e., when it is the object of another sentence, and (3) where continuance of an action is urged and exhorted. The ending in *-u* or *-um* would denote the full conception of an action as having been done, while that in *-i* or *-im* would be little needed and so tend to be lost. Lastly, the construct case of the noun would be represented by the apocopated form of the verbal tense divested of all vowel-terminations, and as the construct case denotes that the noun is subordinated and determined so the apocopated verbal tense denotes the determination of the idea and relation contained in the verb. If the form in *-u* expresses the full verbal conception, the apocopated form expresses the determination of this in a particular way and is therefore peculiarly well fitted to be the historic tense, that tense, namely, which is used for purposes of historical narration. Of course the mimmation would originally have accompanied all the vowel-terminations, but in course of time would have been worn off or only employed for the sake of emphasis. Now Assyrian, like another Sanskrit, is peculiarly valuable in preserving more or less fully all the forms of the ancient Semitic imperfect. First of all, we have the form in -*u* which I propose to call the telic or subjective aorist and which has generally, though for reasons above stated not invariably, the force of a perfect or pluperfect. On this account Dr. Hincks termed it the perfect, and this name may be retained if it is preferred; but I think the one I have proposed is better, not only in order to avoid the confusion which would otherwise arise between this tense-form and the permansive or perfect of other Semitic Grammars, but also because this tense-form does not always bear a perfect signification though we may always trace in its use something of a telic sense. It is generally, if not universally, employed in a relative or conditional clause after *sa* whether used as a pronoun or as an adverb; thus *sa Asur . . . kat-i yusatmikhu* "which Assur had caused my hand to hold," *sa amkhuru-si* "when I had invoked her," *itsbatūni-va emuru* "they had taken and (then) they saw," (when they had taken they saw). Next to the telic aorist will come the aorist of motion or conditional aorist, distinguished by the old accusative termination *a* which we will call the *augment of motion*, though you must carefully bear in mind that it is no suffix, nothing added to the verbal form, but the ancient accusative ending which afterwards came to be dropped in the larger number of instances. I have already stated the three cases in which this conditional aorist would be used, and since it is most commonly employed in Assyrian in the second case, when a condition has to be expressed, perhaps it would be best entitled always the conditional aorist. However it is very frequently employed in the first case, when it is followed by an accusative of the object to which the action of the verb moves forward; but the third sense, that of the cohortative, to which this form of the imperfect is restricted in Hebrew, is never found in Assyrian in the indicative mood. Examples of its use occur in almost every inscription; thus we have *yutsalla'a beluti-ya* "he submitted to my lordship," *icnusa ana neri-ya* "he submitted to my yoke," *sa epusa* "which I made" (not "had made"), *aslula* "I carried off," where though no accusative follows, the idea of motion contained in the verb required this form in -*a*. This accusatival form in -*a* is not confined to the aorist but is also found in the imperative and precative (of which more further on). Here of course it has the cohortative sense which it bears in Hebrew in the case of the indicative.

As has been said, the form of the tense most frequently met with in the inscriptions is the apocopated or construct aorist; or, as it may be called from its frequency in historical narration, the aorist simply. Perhaps one reason for its obtaining the preponderance over other forms lies in its brevity, and consequent aptitude to denote vigour or reality, like the jussive in Arabic and Hebrew. At all events it tended more and more to banish the longer and more original forms and to become the type of the verb.

I need not say much of the paragogic or energetic aorist which retained the mimmation and adapted it to the expression of energy and decision. Of course the mimmation might follow either one of the case-vowels, as *abnum* " I built," *uselam* " I caused to ascend," *usarrikhim* " I consecrated," and could be attached to the imperative and precative. It is more especially prevalent in the Babylonian dialect. Nor need I say much of the very rare termination in -*i* which meets us in *amdakhitsi* " I fought," and *uracsi* " I bound," which has been altogether lost in Arabic prose where the other three aorist-forms are still preserved.

Hitherto we have not come across any deviations on the part of the Assyrian verb from the principles of Semitic grammar. The appropriation of the several forms of the Assyrian aorist to denote different modifications of the conception that underlies it flows naturally from the primary origin of these forms, and corresponds to what we find in other Semitic languages, notably Arabic. Except in the case of the telic aorist, and even here to a less degree than in the Hebrew pluperfect, any temporal signification of the verb is wholly absent; the different significations attached to the different forms are purely relational. Consequently we must treat the Assyrian aorist with its various subdivisions as one whole, like the various forms of the Arabic imperfect, and consider the special meanings which use and age set apart for each of these various forms as so many conventional distinctions. But the case is quite different when we turn to another tense which the Assyrian grammar has elaborated under the influence of Accadian. The latter language, as we learn from the bilingual Grammars of Assur-bani-pal, possessed two tenses, one the aorist formed by prefixing the pronouns to the root, as *in-gin* " he established," the other the present formed by adding a short vowel (as is even now the case in Tibetan) to the final consonant of the root, as *in-gin-e* " he establishes." The Accadian, therefore, distinguished between present and past time, and as the educated classes of Assyria were instructed in the literature of Accad from their earliest youth and constantly required to translate Accadian texts into their own language, it was inevitable that the distinction between present and past time should take such a hold of their mind as to impress itself upon their own language. Now they already had a machinery for the purpose ready to hand. Besides the ordinary form of the aorist *iscun* there was another longer form which interpolated a third vowel upon which the accent fell, producing *isaccin* (i.e., *isácin*). Assyrian was not alone among the Semitic languages in possessing this second form. We find it also in Æthiopic, and in Æthiopic as in Assyrian it was preserved into the days of literature for exactly the same reason, namely that foreign intercourse had originated among both people a verbal conception which was not provided for in the Semitic verb. Now it is a law of language that when the mind wants to express a new idea which it has struck out it seizes upon some previously existing form or word, appropriates the new idea to it, and so creates a special symbol for the idea which has to be expressed. This kind of process is continually going on in the case of synonymes. Two words are in use in a language meaning precisely the same thing; but in course of time one of them is given a new shade of signification, a distinction is then made between them, and the language has gained a new addition. Thus there was a time when the two terminations of Latin comparatives in *-or* and *-us* were convertible; but about the period when the classical language began to be formed a distinction came to be introduced between them, and while *-or* was set apart for the masculine and feminine, *-us* was restricted to the neuter. So, too, Assyrian and Æthiopic both possessed two interchangeable forms of the aorist or imperfect, *iscun* and *isaccin*, but when the need arose of distinguishing between past and present time *iscun* was taken to denote the past, and *isaccin* to denote the present. The distinction was systematically carried out by the Assyrian throughout all the conjugations. These did not possess a shorter form answering to *iscun*, but only the longer form *isaccin*, the third vowel of which might be either *a*, *i*, or *u*, just as the second vowel of the aorist Kal might be either of these vowels. The custom of the language, however, decided that the first of these vowels, *a*, should be confined to the present in the derived conjugations, and only the other two, *i* and more rarely *u*, should be permissible for the aorist. This distinction in the significance of the two vowels was probably determined by the analogy of the Aphel of concave verbs, where *yucin* naturally represented the shorter form *iscun* (the first two radicals *c-v* being agglutinated together) and *yucân* or *yuca'an* stood for *yucáyan* (or *yucáyin*). In Kal, the third vowel of the present continued to the last to be indifferently *a*, *i*, or *u*, though *i* came to be most generally used. Now and then this *i* seems to have affected the preceding vowel changing it to *i*, so that we have *imezzir* instead of *imazzir*, as was instanced when we were engaged upon the conjugations. Thus in Assyrian the verb came to possess besides a Kal aorist, *iscun* " he made," a Kal present, *isaccin* " he makes," and this tense distinction was kept up throughout the remaining conjugations. It is somewhat remarkable that it was this very form *isaccin* which was adopted by Æthiopic to form what Ludolf calls a present (*yĕgábĕr*); and the so-called sub-Semitic dialects of northern Africa, more or less connected with Æthiopic, preserve to this day the tense distinction both in form and meaning which we find in Assyrian. You will meet with abundant instances of the present tense in the inscriptions, in fact every inscription of any length is pretty certain to furnish you with some; while the bilingual tablets are generally careful to translate the Accadian present by the Assyrian present. Indeed the Accadian has given us the best proof we can have that the distinction between *iscun* and *isaccin* was kept up in the other conjugations besides Kal by a distinction of vowel in the last syllable, the same present form answering both to *isaccin* and *yusaccan*. Thus the grammatical tablets lithographed in *W. A. I.* II, pl. 11, render *in-kur* by *yunacir* and *yusanni* " he hated," and *in-kur-ri* by *yunaccar* and *yusanna* " he hates," just as they render *in-lal* by *is-kul* " he weighed," and *in-lal-e* by *isakal* " he weighs." Here, again, we have an example of the usefulness of Accadian to the decipherer, and the assistance afforded him by the possibility of comparing two languages together.

Now since both *iscun* and *isaccin* were originally but variant forms of the same imperfect tense, it follows that *isaccin* also must have originally terminated in the mimmation or a vowel. Hence we should have *isaccinum* or *isaccinu*, *isaccinim* or *isaccini*, *isaccinam* or *isaccina*, just as we have corresponding forms for *iscun*. *Isaccin* is as much a contracted apocopated form as *iscun*, but owing to its length it tended to lose its terminations much more readily than *iscun*. Consequently the mimmation, at least in the northern Assyrian dialect as distinguished from the southern Babylonian, has quite disappeared in the case of this (present) form; so also has the termination in -*i*. The termination in -*a* is sometimes used when motion or condition is implied, in fact under the same circumstances as those under which it is found with the aorist; though naturally the conditional aorist is more frequently employed for this purpose than the conditional present. The termination in -*u* had been appropriated in the case of the aorist to denote a slight modification in the meaning of that tense; in the case of the present also, but more persistently and clearly, it was appropriated to denote a modification of meaning. Wherever we meet with the form *isaccinu* instead of *isaccin* we always find it with a distinctly *future* sense; hundreds of examples might be collected, which you will easily verify for yourselves. Once (*W. A. I.* I., 16, col. 8, l. 71) we have *ikhatsatsa* "he will chip," in the place of *i-kha-tsa-tsu*, followed by *va* "and;" but the explanation of this *a* instead of *u* must be sought in the euphonic law which assimilated the final vowel of the tense to those which preceded and followed it. Similarly we occasionally find *u* changed into *av* before a *va*, as at Behistun, 15, 30, *it-bav* "they came," or in the case of nouns like *'ablav* for *'ablu* "son" (Borsippa, ii. 16).

I have dwelt thus long upon the subject of the tenses, because it is one of the most important and characteristic parts of Assyrian grammar. Let us now pass on to the moods. The indicative has already been implicitly discussed, since all the tenses we have been considering belong to that mood. The subjunctive, again, will not detain us long. It can hardly be called a distinct mood, as it is simply formed by the enclitic *ni* added either to the perfect or to the permansive, and it follows a relative or such particles as *ci* "when." The enclitic *ni* comes after the possessive pronominal suffix, as *abilu-sina-ni* "I have possessed them," *ikabu'-su-ni* "he has called it;" but when there is no pronominal suffix the enclitic is attached immediately to the verb, as *ci utsbacu-ni* "when I was stopping." Of far more importance is the precative formed by prefixing *li* or *lu* to the aorist. The precative is generally used only in the third person; occasionally, however, it is found in the first person, and once or twice in the second. Thus we get *li-ru-ur* "may he curse," *liscun* "may he place," *lu-rab-bis* "may he enlarge," *lu-tir* "may he

restore," *lu-ub-lu-udh* " may I live," *lu-uc-su-ud* " may I obtain," *lu-us-bi-im*
" may I be satisfied with," *lu-ti-ip-pis* " mayest thou make," *lis-su-u-ni* " may
they carry away." The prefix is *lu* whenever *u* is a performative of the
conjugation, and seems always to be employed with the first person. This
lu must be carefully distinguished from the conjunction *lū* or *lu-u* which
denotes past time and never amalgamates with the verb. You will find
many instances of the latter particle in the famous cylinder inscription of
Tiglath-Pileser I. Instead of the second person of the precative the imperative is employed; indeed the imperative is wholly confined to the second
person. The second person masculine singular Kal presents us with the
root of the verb in its simplest and barest form, the three radicals being
divided from one another by two vowels which must be alike but may vary
according to the last vowel of the third person singular of the aorist Kal.
Thus *iscun* with *u* is the third singular aorist Kal; the imperative therefore
is *sucun* " place thou," but *irkhits* " he inundated," with *i*, makes the imperative *rikhits*, and *itsbat* " he took," with *a*, makes *tsabat*. In the weak verbs
the imperative undergoes many transformations. Verbs פ״נ lose the initial
nasal, hence *nāmaru* " to see " makes *umur*, *nāpalu* " to throw down,"*apal*,
and *nādanu* " to give," *idin*. Verbs, the first radical of which is *u* or *i*, lose
it altogether, so that from *uladu* " to beget," comes *lid*, and from *iniku* " to
suckle," *nik;* verbs פ״א also sometimes suffer the same loss; thus whereas
ācalu " to eat " makes *acul*, from *āsabu* " to swell " we have *sib* (as if from
usabu) as well as *asib*. Shaphel assumes the vowel *ŭ* after it, instead of
before it, as in the indicative, and so produces the form *suscin*. As I have
remarked before, the mimmation and termination in *a* are often preserved
in the imperative and precative, though not the termination in *u*. The
termination in *a*, with its idea of motion, was peculiarly applicable to the
imperative to which it gave a cohortative sense. The last mood of the
Assyrian verb is the infinitive, which like all other infinitives is really
an abstract noun, and must be treated in all respects as one. I need
only say that *sācanu* is the normal or type-form of the Assyrian infinitive,
unless one of the radicals is *e*, when *episu* takes its place. Along with
the infinitive we may notice the participle present or *nomen agentis*, which
has the form *sācinu* in Kal; the other conjugations prefix *mŭ-*. This also
is a noun.

All that now remains is to say a few words on the formation of the numbers, genders, and persons, of the Assyrian tenses. There are three numbers, singular, dual, and plural, though as in the case of the nouns, the dual is but little used. It is only found with dual subjects like *uznā* "the ears," or *sepā* "the feet," and even then the plural is often substituted for it. Like the dual of the noun, the dual of the verb is always characterised by the termination *ā*. The genders also follow the pattern of the noun, and remind us that the Semitic verb was itself originally a noun. There are but two genders, the masculine and the feminine, the latter being distinguished by the vowel *a* (weakened to *i*) or the ending *a(t)*. The first person alone has no feminine. A distinction is made between the person-suffixes of the permansive and the person-suffixes of the aorist. In the permansive they are always affixes, and so far as the first two persons singular are concerned the shortened forms of the personal pronouns. Thus *sacnacu* with *acu* shortened(?) from *anacu* is the first person, *sacnat* with *at* shortened from *atta* the second person masculine. The third person is really the participle active, as in the other Semitic languages, but *without the case-endings;* and this distinction will always tell you whether you are dealing with the third singular of the permansive or the participle present. Thus *sacin* is the permansive, but *sacinu* the participle. The permansive again is used like a verb with an accusative (if it is transitive) and comes at the end of a sentence, and this will serve to distinguish it from the construct state of the participle which precedes the noun it governs. I have already tried to explain how the participle present became transformed into a tense and attached the personal pronouns to itself. The first person of the plural has not been met with. The third person plural and dual end in *ū*, *ă*, and *ā* (as *sacnū*, *sacnă*, *sacnā*). You will observe that the short *i* between the second and third radicals is dropped whenever the word is weighted with an affix. The formation of the permansive, therefore, is simple enough. That of the aorist, however, is much more complex. In this tense the pronouns are prefixed instead of being affixed, though affixes are also used, and they are attached not to the participle present but to what the Aryan grammarians would call a stem. The scheme of the apocopated aorist and present is given at the end of the chapter. To form the conditional aorist or present we must affix *a* to all those persons which end in a consonant, change final *ă* into *ā* (in the third feminine plural), and add *a* to the *u* of the third masculine plural which then becomes *wa*, and, as *w* is not written in Assyrian, *ā* (e.g., *aslulā* for *aslulu-a*). What happens, however, in the case of the second feminine singular? I do not know, as instances of this person are very rare in the inscriptions and I have never come across an example of its use with the conditional *a*-ending. Probably, however, the *a*-vowel was affixed to the *i* in spite of the hiatus, since we find the precative *lusbi'am* "may I be satiated." The termination in *u* followed the pattern of that in *a* except in the third person plural. Here it assumed a form which requires a little explanation. The second and third persons plural of the Assyrian present and aorist are contracted forms and have suffered from the action of phonetic decay. The analogy of the other Semitic dialects shows us that they have dropped a final syllable, being shortened from *tascunūnŭ, tascunānu, iscunūnu* and *iscunānu*, or rather from the mimmated forms of these. Now just as the perfect or telic aorist in -*u* preserves the original ending of the aorist in the singular, so in the plural also it preserves the primitive termination in *ūnu*, the same termination (the last vowel excepted) that we meet with in Hebrew poetry. In fact the perfect aorist is throughout the original Semitic imperfect, and since that imperfect ended in *ūnu(m)* in the second and third persons plural, the perfect aorist also must show the same termination. Instead of *ūnu*, however, we more frequently find *ūni*, the *u*-vowel being weakened to *i* partly for euphony's sake, partly from the action of phonetic decay, partly from the analogy of the ordinary plural-ending in *i*. Hence *ūni* is more common than *ūnu*, and when we meet a plural of this kind formed by means of ⟨𒌋⟩, which, as you know, represents both *nuv* and *niv*, we ought to transliterate it by *niv* rather than by *nuv*. *Una* also is found, though rarely, and probably with a conditional force. The final *v* of *nuv* or *niv* given above must not be regarded as an instance of the mimmation, since the character which contains it is only used before the conjunction *va* "and," and the double *v* simply denotes that the accent is thrown back by the enclitic conjunction upon the short *i* which precedes it, and not upon the long antepenultima. Thus *itsbatūniv-va emuru* "when they had taken they saw," does not stand for *itsbatunim-va* but for *itsbatūni-va*. However examples of the mimmation occur not unfrequently, but generally with an intensive sense. In these mimmated forms we may see the most primitive form of the Semitic imperfect which has branched off in Assyrian into an aorist and a perfect, a present and a future. All that the student has to do is to commit to memory the aorist (or apocopated imperfect) and from this he can form the present by changing *iscun* into *isaccin* in Kal, and by replacing *i* or *u* in the last syllable by *a* in the other conjugations; the perfect and future being further obtained by adding *u* to those persons of the aorist and present which end in a consonant, and *ni* or *nu* to those which end in a vowel.

We have now accomplished the hardest and most important part of our task, the conjugation of the strong or regular verb. When the rules and principles upon which this is founded are once fairly mastered, we may consider that we have broken the backbone of Assyrian grammar and are prepared for attacking the decipherment of the texts. The weak or defective verbs follow the paradigms of the strong verb so far as the phonetic rules of the language allow them do so; and if their forms differ from those of the strong verb it is only because a possible syllable has been lost through transition of one or more of their radicals into a vowel. Before passing on to these weak verbs, however, I must say a few words about letter-change in the conjugation of the strong verb itself, as well as glance hastily at the special subordinate rules which may be peculiar to the several conjugations.

One of the chief causes of letter-change in the conjugation, which often makes the recognition of a familiar form difficult to the beginner, is contraction by the loss of short syllables. Thus short *ĭ* and *ă* are very liable to be dropped, *listalamu* "may they perfect," for instance, may be written *listalmu; taptikidi* "thou overseest," *taptikdi; lissacina* "may they be placed," *lissacna*. Where a double consonant precedes the short vowel, when the vowel is elided, it of course becomes a single one, as *istacnu* for *istaccanu* "they place," *ittalcu* for *ittallicu* "they went." Sometimes, but rarely, the short *ă* of the second syllable of Shaphel disappears, as in *usziz* for *usaziz* "I caused to fix." More perplexing than this contraction of syllables are the results brought about by the action of those phonetic laws, with which we were dealing in a former lecture. When the first radical is *d*, *ts*, *z*, or *s*, the *t* characteristic of the secondary conjugation is assimilated to these letters, so that we have *itstsabat* "he takes," for *itstabat*, *izzacar* "he remembers," for *iztacar*, while *s* changes *t* into *s* and is then assimilated itself, as *issacan* "he places," for *istacan*, *assarap* "I burn," for *astarap*. But a double letter, you will remember, may be omitted in writing; and so we may have *aśarap* instead of *aśśarap*, *izacar* instead of *izzacar*. This omission of a double letter is a constant source of confusion, and often makes it quite impossible to decide with certainty under what particular head a certain form has to be referred. To take *izacar* above, it may just as well be Kal present as Iphteal present for *izzacar* (*iztacar*) or even Niphal present. In the case of Pael the performative *u* always informs us of the form even though the double letter be unexpressed; but a controversy has arisen over the form *yucin* in concave verbs, whether it is an Aphel or (as Dr. Hincks maintained) a Pael for *yuccin*. The fact, however, that we always find *yucin* and never *yuccin* sufficiently determines that it is an Aphel form. Other letter-changes which frequently transform the appearance of a verb are the change of *s* into *l* before a dental, which generally makes Istaphal an Iltaphal, the assimilation of a nasal to the following consonant (the consonant sometimes having originally been *m*, e.g., *ikhkhir*), and the change of *t* into *dh* and *d* after gutturals and nasals, as *ikdharib* for *iktarib* " he approached," *amdakhits* for *amtakhits* " I fought." These letter-changes do not always take effect; we find *ustascan* for instance, as well as *ultascan*, *indin* as well as *iddin*, *amtakhits* as well as *amdakhits*.

Every rule, it has been said, admits of an exception, and no generalisation can take account of all the details. The general rules relative to the Assyrian conjugation which we have been considering must be supplemented by a few remarks which most fitly come under the head of the several conjugations. Thus to begin with Kal, the vowel of the last syllable of the apocopated or construct aorist may be either *a*, *i*, or *u*. Verbs which have *a* are mostly transitives, while by far the largest number of verbs have *u*. Many verbs, however, admit all three vowels, euphony alone deciding which of the three is preferred. Thus in the same inscription we find *itsbat* " he took," but *itsbutu* " they took," where the vowel has been assimilated to the vowel of the termination, and elsewhere we have *epus*, " I made," by the side of *epis*. In a few cases a distinction of meaning has grown up between forms with *a* and *u* which were originally identical; thus *amkhar* is " I received," *amkhur* " I increased." Another point to be observed is the change of the characteristic of the first person singular of the Kal aorist (*a*) into *e* in the Babylonian dialect; *aśnik*, for instance, becoming *eśnik*. *E* here will be equivalent to the Hebrew *seghol* in words like *ekdhol*. In the northern dialect of Assyria verbs פ״א might undergo the same change; thus we find *ecul* "I ate" as well as *acul*. We have already had to notice (p. 82) the preference for the neutral vowel *e* shown by the verbal forms in Assyrian; this preference is especially marked in the Babylonian dialect, where, for example, the Iphtaneal *irtaniddi* "he added" appears as *er-ten-iddi*. Another Iphtaneal form which requires explanation is *atnimmus* "I departed." This stands for *atanimmus* from מוש, the characteristic *tan* being inserted before the first radical in accordance with the rule for concave verbs laid down above. A verb which frequently takes the place of *atnimmus* in the inscriptions is *attusir*. This is an Ittaphal (for *antusir*) from וסר "to turn" or "depart." Before leaving the strong verb I would draw your attention to the interesting change of signification in the Iphtaal of the verb *halacu* "to go." The Pael *hallacu* has a causative sense "to make go," while the Iphtaal *attallacu* serves as the middle voice of the Pael meaning "to be driven to go," "to walk," or "march."

I now come to the defective or weak verbs, in which we have to trace the action of the special laws which interfere with the general scheme of conjugation as laid down for the strong verb. Let us first take verbs פ״ן. Little need be said about these, as they are regular throughout except in the imperative, where the initial *n* is dropped, so that we get *umur* "be visible," *idin* "give," and *apal* "fall down," according to the vowel of the aorist. The nasal is generally assimilated to the following letter; sometimes it may be resolved into *m* before *b* or *p*, and *n* before a dental.

More has to be said about verbs, one of whose radicals is a vowel. They constitute the hardest part of Assyrian grammar, and the attempts made to distinguish their forms have been singularly contradictory. The reason of this lies in the fact that the Assyrians themselves did not discriminate very accurately between these different classes of verbs (verbs ל״ה excepted). The same root was sometimes used as a verb פ״א, sometimes as a verb פ״ו, sometimes even as a verb פ״ע, a verb פ״ן, a concave verb, or a verb ל״ה. Hence the unsatisfactory character of the endeavours to draw up clear and definite paradigms of the three classes of verbs פ״א, פ״ו, פ״י. The question, however, is rather one for advanced scholars than for beginners, and, so long as the paradigms given in my *Elementary Assyrian Grammar*, are kept well in sight, one of little practical importance. Those who wish to see the question fully discussed and worked out may turn to my *Assyrian Grammar*, p. 86. I have there summed up the results of a careful examination of the inscriptions upon this point, and noted that "it was only at a comparatively late period that the Semites came to distinguish between the forms which a so-called biliteral root might take. The sharp divisions of the Hebrew grammarians are the results of later reflexion. Assyrian has hardly entered upon this discriminating stage: hence the same biliteral root appears under different forms, which a grammar (though not necessarily the decipherer) has to assign to different triliteral stems. From *dhabu*, for instance, we have forms which presuppose *dhavabu* and *dhabu'u*, from *canu* forms which presuppose *cavanu, cananu, nacanu, acanu, ucanu,* and *icinu.*" One of the commonest of verbs is *ātsu* "to go out," but you will occasionally come across forms which must be derived not from *ātsu* but from *ūtsu.* Other forms would seem to point to the first radical being *e ;* indeed in Shaphel, the first radical always becomes *e* whether it were originally *e* or *a* or *i.* In the Babylonian dialect, again, verbs פ״א are very often treated as though they were verbs פ״ע, and even in the northern Assyrian we have indifferently *ecul* and *acul* "I ate," *elih* and *alih* "I exalt." So, too, verbs פ״א and verbs פ״י are liable to be confounded, and, as in Hebrew, verbs פ״י readily pass into verbs פ״ץ. Perhaps the most curious point is the confusion that exists between verbs פ״א and verbs פ״ן and which accounts for the loss of the initial in the imperatives of the latter verbs. The conjugation of verbs פ״ה is properly kept quite distinct from that of these other verbs, and if they seem identical it is only through a fault of writing. Now and then the initial *h* is written as *ahbid* "I destroyed," but more generally it is dropped and replaced by the doubling of the second consonant. Thus instead of *ahlic* "I went," we have *allic*, and this reduplication of the second radical is quite sufficient to mark off verbs of this class from any others. But the tendency of the Assyrian scribes to save time and trouble by omitting to express a double letter in writing frequently causes *alic* to appear in the texts in the place of *allic.* So by what I have called a fault of writing the verbs which begin with *h* are confounded with those which begin with '*a.*

The concave verbs, those namely which have a semi-consonant passing into a vowel as middle radical, will next occupy our attention. The type-forms of these which are given in the bilingual grammatical tablets are extremely valuable as showing that the Assyrian scribes, at a time when the language was still a living one, and no grammatical theories had prejudiced the minds of its speakers, believed instinctively in the triliteralism of Semitic speech. These concave roots have been one of the sheet-anchors of the advocates of the modern hypothesis which would resolve Semitic triliterals into more primitive biliterals and assimilate the Semitic family to the Aryan family of languages. Certainly when we come across forms like *itar* and *itur* we are tempted to think that here at least we are dealing with a monosyllabic root. But just as קָם in Hebrew stands for קָוַם so *itar* in Assyrian stands for *itavar* or *itayar;* and the Assyrian itself not unfrequently expressed this fact by substituting a double initial consonant for the lost medial one and saying *ittar* and *ittur.* You will find that these reduplicated forms of Kal are extremely common in the inscriptions, and bear witness to the unchangeable conviction of the language that it was based upon triliteral roots. When, again, we turn to the infinitive or type-form set down in the bilingual tablets, we find not *taru* or *turu* but *ta-a-ru,* *ta'aru,* i.e., *tawaru,* the Assyrians having no other way of expressing *w* in writing. So, too, the participle present of Kal is *ta'iru,* *ca'inu* for *tawinu* or *tayinu;* and the permansive of כון is given as *ca'inacu* for *cawinacu,* where the short *i* has been preserved instead of being lost as in *sacnacu* (for *sacĭnacu*) owing to its being lengthened by assimilation to *w* changed into *y.* Dr. Schrader once objected that *ca'inacu* could not be a permansive since *ai* could not in that case stand in the first syllable; but his objection rested on an oversight; the first syllable is not *ai,* but *a,* and the second is *i.* That striving after vocalic euphony in which the Assyrian may possibly have been influenced by the Accadian, caused, however, the *ĭ* of the second syllable to become *a* and this occasioned the loss of the hiatus and the contraction of the two *a*'s into *ā.* Hence besides *ca'inacu* we also find *cāmacu* " I burn." In two of the other conjugations the permansive or perfect takes a form peculiar to verbs of this class. Instead of the ordinary Pael permansive after the type of *karradacu,* *karrad,* we have one with a passive signification which is identical in form with the participle passive of Kal. The latter takes the form *dīcu* " slain," *cīnu* " established," like Aramaic; and the Pael permansive which corresponds is *cin* and *dic.* Thus in Behistun 17, R, we have *mîti* "he is dead," like the Hebrew מֵת, and the Assyrian translation of an ancient Accadian threshing song runs as follows: *al-la-cā bir-ca-ai la-a ni-khā se-pa-ai* "my knees march, my feet rest not." In Sm. *A.* 24, 6, again, we read *at-tu-ni a-sa-ba-ni mi-i-nu* "as for us (our) seats are numbered."

The other conjugation to which I referred is the Palel, possessed by all concave verbs. Here the third person plural is *cunnu'u*, which translates the Accadian aorist causative *ib-tan-gubbu-s* (*W. A. I.* II., 15. 3); and *cullu* "they are holding" (NR., 11, 26, Behistun 34, R), must accordingly be referred to a concave verb rather than to כלה. What the first person singular would be it is hard to say, and no example of it has yet been discovered.

There are some other noticeable points connected with these concave verbs. (1) Instead of a Niphal and Ittaphel they possess only a Niphalel and Ittaphalel, doubling the last radical, and though we find instances of Pael, Iphtaal, Shaphel, and Istaphal, yet Palel, Iphtalel, Shaphalel, and Istaphalel are more common. As I have just assumed, the double consonant of *cunnu* and *cullu* given above implies that they belong to a Palel rather than to a Pael and is not merely a mark of the length of the preceding vowel. (2) They possess also an Aphel, which it is somewhat difficult in many cases to distinguish from a Pael. Dr. Schrader believes that *yuca'an* which I have made the present of Aphel really belongs to Pael, and accordingly reads it *yucayan* for *yucayyan*. In this case *yucan* would be the present of Aphel. But I have not come across any clear instance of the existence of the latter form, while *yu'uccan* and *yuccan* are met with; and these two forms can only be referred to Pael. (3) The position of the dental in Iphteal and Iphtaal, before the first radical instead of after it, agrees with the usage of Hebrew, Aramaic, Ethiopic, and the fifth and sixth conjugations of Arabic, and tends to show that in Assyrian also as well as in the cognate idioms, Tiphel was older than Iphteal. It is one of the rules of language that primitive forms which have been supplanted by others are preserved only rarely and exceptionally. The general tendency of the language to insert the *t* after the first radical invaded even the concave verbs, and we find *uctin* "I established," from כון and *astil* and *ultil* from סול "I raised," as well as *itbu* "he came," *itcun* "he established." (4) As in process of time the original three consonants of these concave verbs came to be more and more worn away into vowels, and the old triliterals to become biliteral monosyllables, the instinctive endeavour of the language to restore the primitive triliteralism which showed itself in one direction by creating a Niphalel and a Palel, produced intensive and iterative forms, which we may term Papel and Palpel conjugations, like *gargaru* "to rush with a noise," *rakraku* "to be very yellow." Perhaps the same-consciousness that the original inheritance of triliteral roots had been given up in the case of these verbs was the cause of that frequent reduplication of their final radicals to denote the accentuation of the preceding syllable which we find in the texts. It is possible that this may be the reason of the double consonant in *cullu* and *cunnū*, it is certainly the case with such forms as *uctanna-su* "I establish it," or those which we meet with in an interesting passage in the Astrological Tablets[1] which seems to allude to a conquest of Chaldea by the Elamites, and an occupation of the country for thirty years. We there read *Bilu ana mat Elamti illac* "Bel to Elam goes;" *cibitta ina silasā sanāti duc-tū yut-tar-ru* "at last after thirty years the smitten are restored;" *ili rabi itti su-nu i-tur-ru* "the great gods with them returned." Before dismissing the concave verbs, I may mention that verbs with medial ה sometimes are treated as concaves, though in this case the first radical is repeated to make up for the loss of the *h*. Thus instead of *inhar* we have *innar* "it shines."

Verbs לא״, לה״, לי״, לי״, all take the same forms in Assyrian (except in the aorist and imperative Kal); verbs לה״, indeed, do not appear to exist at all, the aspirate having in all cases been reduced to a vowel. Verbs לע״ which may be classed with the others for all essential purposes have *e* in the last syllable, as *is-me-e* or *is-ma-e* or *is-me* "he heard," and in the more correct texts this *e* is preserved throughout as *isme'a* "he heard," *is-me'-u* "they hear;" but more often we find it coalescing with the vowel following (*ismā, ismū, ismu'u*) and so disappearing altogether. In the present aorist and imperative Kal verbs לא״ and לי״ end in *i'* as *akbi'* "I called," *tagabbi'* "thou sayest," *khidhi* "sin thou," unless *u* followed, when *i* and *u* combined into *ū* as in the plural *ikbū* "they called,"[2]

---

[1] *W. A. I.* III., 61. 2. 22.

[2] The vowel *ĭ*, however, is preserved in the older and fuller form of the 3rd plural, as in *ikbi'uni*, "they have called."

or the future *tagabbū* "thou wilt call." You will recollect how frequently 'a passes into *i*, ראש for instance becoming *ris(u)*. Verbs ל״י, on the other hand, have *u'* in the last syllable, as *abnu'* "I built," except in the second person feminine or in those forms which terminate in *a*. In the other conjugations the present always ends in '*a*, the aorist in *i'*. Verbs ל״ה must be classed with verbs ל״א and ל״י, though the greater number of them have become ל״י. Hebrew has been more conservative than Assyrian in this respect and preserved the final aspirate which we no longer find in the language of Nineveh. In comparing Assyrian and Hebrew roots, therefore, we must bear in mind that verbs which end in a vowel in the one language will end in ה in the other. Thus the Assyrian *banu* is the Hebrew בנה. Let me point out one thing more. Verbs ל״א drop the final vowel and radical in the second person masculine singular of the imperative, herein differing from verbs ל״ה, ל״י, ל״י and ל״ע which end in -*ĭ*. Thus נשא gives us *nas* "lift thou up," but שתה *siti* "drink."

The last group of defectives that need be noticed are those which contain *e*. Now *e* in Assyrian is always a vowel, often interchanging with *i*; but although thus worn down to a mere vocalic pronunciation it yet preserved enough of its original character to make its presence felt and to work certain changes upon the accompanying letters. I have already said all that need be observed about verbs ל״ע; and since verbs ע״ע follow all the peculiarities of concave verbs, all that remains to notice are verbs פ״ע. The *e* almost always shows itself in verbs of this kind, and the student, therefore, need seldom be puzzled as to whether or not a word before him contains this letter. An exception occurs only where the preformative *u;* precedes the *e*, which coalesces with it in Assyrian, forming *ū;* in the Babylonian dialect, however, *e* is simply assimilated without coalescing, and thus forms *u'u;* so that whereas *ullā* "I raised," is the Assyrian form of the Pael of עלה (here, it will be noticed, with a causative sense), *u'ullā* is the Babylonian form. But the Babylonian dialect often disguises the radical in another case, that is, in the third person aorist and perfect Kal, where instead of the Assyrian *ebus*, *ebusu*, the Babylonian has *ibus* and *ibusu*. Not always, however; sometimes we find the fuller, more correct form *e'ibus* where the radical and preformative are separate, though they have changed places. An exception occurs, again, in Niphal, where *e* is replaced by a reduplication of the second radical producing *ibbis;* and as the reduplication is so frequently left unnoticed in writing *ibis* not rarely meets us in the texts. Of course, the substitution of *e* for *a* in the first person singular of verbs like *ecul* "I ate," or *esnik,* must be carefully distinguished from cases in which it is one of the radicals of the root. Before quitting the subject of verbs which contain *e* I must refer to a modification of the conjugations of the regular verb in which *e* or its substitute *i* intrudes itself between the second and third radical. Dr. Hincks proposed to add a new conjugation "of which," as he said, "the first aorist is *'upekil,*" a form of which the inscriptions present us with numerous examples, e.g., *usepic* "I heaped up," *unecis* "I cut off." But further acquaintance with the language has made it clear that most, if not all, of the conjugations furnish similar forms, as I have pointed out on an earlier occasion. It is evident, therefore, that *usepic, unecis* and other words as *yunicim* (quoted when we were dealing with the Pael) belong to the Pael conjugation; and that the reduplication of the second radical has been dropped or perhaps replaced by the modification of the vowel. It would seem that these *'ayin*-forms (as we may call them) were confined to verbs which had *i* as the vowel of the last syllable of the aorist, and the best explanation that can be afforded of them is that in them we have another instance of that vowel harmony which has met us before, and that the *e* or *i* of the second syllable is caused by its assimilation in sound to the third. We may parallel it by a word like *cherish* for *charish* in English.

I cannot close our review of the verbs without alluding to the quadri-literals and quinqueliterals of which there are not very many in Assyrian. The most common are *palcitu* "to cross," *sakhparu* "to overthrow," *parsidu* "to pursue," *kharpasu* "to be vehement," *naparacu* "to be broken." The latter verb, however, is really the Niphal of *paracu,* and by the side of *sakhparu* and *parsidu* we find *sakhapu* and *parasu.* Thus *ipparsū* occurs as well as *ipparsudu, iskhup* as well as *iskhupar,* and though *ipparsū* may be explained as a contracted form of *ipparsudu,* (*d* being dropped, as in *sisu* "six," and *essu* "new" from חדש) the same explanation can hardly hold good of *iskhup.* One point has to be noticed about these pluriliterals, and that is that almost always one of their radicals is an *r* or an *l.* Now there are indubitable instances in which *r* in Semitic words has been an insertion to facilitate pronunciation; thus *Darmeshek* is the Syriac form of Damascus which occurs also in I Chr. xviii. 5, 6, but the Assyrian *Dimasku* shows that the Hebrew is the more correct form of the name. So, too, the Hebrew כִּסֵּא " throne," is the Assyrian *cussu*, borrowed from the Accadian *guza*; but Syriac and Arabic give us *curs'ya* and Aramaic *corsai*. It is quite possible, therefore, that some of these quadriliterals have been produced in the same way. This, however, cannot have been the case with many of them, *ipparsudu* for example; and when we find the Hebrew צְפַרְדֵּעַ *tsephardea'*, compounded of צָפַר " to croak," and רְדַע " a marsh," or אלם reduced to the Arabic لَمَّ we seem forced to the conclusion that some at least of the pluriliterals are compounds, and that phonetic decay has worn them down into their shortened form.

We may now congratulate ourselves upon our safe passage through the main part of Assyrian grammar. So far as the accidence is concerned, there is little left. The particles need not detain us long, since they are rather to be learnt by heart than discoursed upon. The prepositions especially must be committed to memory. Some of the most common of these take shapes unfamiliar to the Semitic student; but it must be remembered that the same is also the case in Ethiopic where prepositions like *diba* " on," *mesla* "with" have a singularly un-Semitic appearance. *Itti*, אֵת "with," *ci*, *adi* and *eli* are, as you see, identical with the corresponding Hebrew prepositions, and the only ones that really look strange are *ana*, *ina*, *istu* or *ultu* and *assu*. I shall not here hazard a conjecture as to the origin of *ana* and *ina*; judging from the analogy of the other prepositions we should infer that they were derived from substantives and not from pronouns or " pronominal roots," that last resource of etymological despair. *Istu* or *ultu* (for *ustu*) is equally obscure, but it seems to have a feminine termination and to have ע for first radical; comp. Ethiopic *wĕsta*. Most of the other prepositions bear their derivations on the face. Thus *pan* is the " face," *nir* "the foot," *tik* " the rear," *arci*, "the back." An interesting confirmation of the derivation of the Hebrew לְ from לוה is afforded by the fact that the Assyrian *li* is contracted from the more common *liviti*. As regards the conjunctions, special care must be directed to the use of the copulative *va* " and." Verbs belonging to the same sentence and therefore completing the same idea, and even belonging to different sentences but dependent on the same main idea, are coupled by the enclitic conjunction *vă*, which throws back the accent on the preceding syllable, even though this is short (e.g., *-unĭ*). The accentuation of this syllable is then ordinarily denoted by doubling the *v*. If *u* precedes, the *v* sometimes assimilates and forms *w* which is dropped in writing, so that we get *aslulā* " they carried off" for *aslulu-va*. This occasionally happens even if no *u* goes before as in *sukalul-a* for *sukalul-va*. This *a* which represents the shortened *vă* must be carefully distinguished from the *a* of the conditional aorist. It is, however, sufficient to show us that the conjunction was really an enclitic, and thus contrasted with the Hebrew prefixed ‎וַ

PARADIGMS OF THE ASSYRIAN VERB.

THE STRONG VERB.

KAL.

PERMANSIVE (or Perfect).			PRESENT.
Sing. 3. *masc.*	sacin		isaccin (isácin) *he places* (*also* isaccun *and* isaccan)
	fem.	sacnāt	tasaccin (tasácin)
	2. *masc.*	sacnat	tasaccin (tasácin)
	fem.	sacnat	tasaccini (tasácini)
	1.	sacnacu *or* sacnac	asaccin (asàcin)
Plu. 3. *masc.*	sacnuni, sacnu		isaccinu (isácinu)
	fem.	[sacnāni], sacnā	isaccina (isácina)
	2. *masc.*	sacnatunu	tasaccinu (tasàcinu)
	fem.	[sacnatina]	tasaccina (tasácina)
	1.	[sacnani ?]	nisaccin (nisácin)
Dual. 3.	sacnā		isaccinā (isácinā)

AORIST (Construct Aorist).			FUTURE.	PERFECT OR PLUPERFECT (Subjective Aorist).
Sing. 3. *masc.*	iscun *he placed* (*also* irkhits *and* itsbat)		isacinu (isácinu)	iscunu
	fem.	tascun	tasaccinu	tascunu
	2. *masc.*	tascun	tasaccinu	tascunu
	fem.	tascuni	[tasaccini ?]	[tascuni ?]
	1.	ascun	asaccinu	ascunu
Plu. 3. *masc.*	iscunu		isaccinuni	iscununi
	fem.	iscuna	isaccinani	iscunani
	2. *masc.*	tascuna	tasaccinuni	tascununi
	fem.	tascuna	tasaccinani	tascunani
	1.	niscun	nisaccinu	niscunu
Dual. 3.	iscunā		[isaccinā ?]	[iscunā ?]

IMPERATIVE.		PRECATIVE.		INFINITIVE.
Sing. 2. *masc.* sucun		*Sing.* 3.	liscun	sacānu *to dwell*
	rikhits		lirkhits	rakhatsu *to inundate*
	tsabat		litsbat	tsabatu *to seize*
fem. sucini *or* sucni		2.	lutascun	
		1.	luscun	
Plu. 2. *masc.* sucinu *or* sucnu		*Plu.* 3. *masc.* liscunu		PARTICIPLE.
fem. sucina *or* sucna		*fem.* liscuna		sācinu *dwelling*

IPHTEAL.

PERMANSIVE (or Perfect).		PRESENT.	AORIST.
Sing. 3. *masc.* sitcun		istacan *or* iltacan	istacin *or* iltacin, iptekid
fem. sitcunat		tastacan	tastacin
2. *masc.* sitcunat		tastacan	tastacin
fem. sitcunat		tastacani, tastacni	tastacini, tastacni
1.	sitcunacu	astacan	astacin
Plu. 3. *masc.* sitcunu		istacanu	istacinu, istacnu
fem. sitcuna		istacana	īstacina
2. *masc.* [sitcuntunu]		tastacanu	tastacinu
fem. [sitcuntina]		tastacana	tastacina
1.	?	nistacan	nistacin
Dual. 3.	[sitcunā]	istacanā	istacinā

IMPERATIVE.	PRECATIVE.	INFINITIVE.
Sing. 2. *masc.* sitcin, satcin	*Sing.* 3. listacan, liptekid	sitcunu
fem. sitcini	1. lustacan	PARTICIPLE.
Plu. 2. *masc.* sitcinu	*Plu.* 3. *masc.* listacanu	mustacanu *or* multacanu
fem. sitcina	3. *fem.* listacana	muptekidu

NIPHAL.

PERMANSIVE (or Perfect).		PRESENT.	AORIST.
Sing. 3. *masc.* nascun		issacan	issacin, issacun
fem. [nascunat]		tassacan	tassacan, tassacun
2. *masc.* [nascunat]		tassacan	tassacin, tassacun
fem. [nascunat]		tassacani, tassacni	tassacini, tassacni, tassacuni
1.	[nascunacu]	assacan	assacin, tassacun
Plu. 3. *masc.* nascunu		issacanu, issacnu	issacinu, issacnu, issacunu
fem. nascuna		issacana, issacna	issacina, issacna, issacuna
2. *masc.* [nascuntunu]		tassacanu, tassacnu	tassacinu, tassacnu, tassacunu
fem. [nascuntina]		tassacana, tassacna	tassacina, tassacna, tassacuna
1.	?	nissacan	nissacin, nissacun
Dual. 3.	[nascunā]	[issacanā]	[issacinā]

IMPERATIVE.	PRECATIVE.	INFINITIVE.	PARTICIPLE.
Sing. 2. *masc.* nascin	*Sing.* 3. lissacin	nascānu	munascinu
fem. nascini	1. lussacin		
Plu. 2. *masc.* nascinu	*Plu.* 3. *masc.* lissacinu, lissacnu		
fem. nascina	*fem.* lissacina, lissacna		

ITTAPHAL.

PERMANSIVE (or Perfect).	PRESENT.	AORIST.
Sing. 3. *masc.* nastecun	ittascan	ittascin, ittascun
etc., etc.	etc., etc.	etc., etc.

IMPERATIVE.	PRECATIVE.	INFINITIVE.	PARTICIPLE.
Sing. 2. *masc.* nitascin (?)	*Sing.* 3. littascin	nastacānu	muttascinu
etc., etc.	etc., etc.		muttascanu

PAEL.

PERMANSIVE (or Perfect).	PRESENT.	AORIST.
Sing. 3. *masc.* saccan	yŭsaccan (yusacan)	yŭsaccin
fem. saccanat	tŭsaccan	tŭsaccin
2. *masc.* [saccanat]	tŭsaccan	tŭsaccin
fem. [saccanat]	tŭsaccani, tŭsacni	tŭsaccini, tŭsacni
1. saccanacu	'ūsaccan	'ūsaccin
Plu. 3. *masc.* saccanu, sacnu	yŭsaccanu, yŭsacnu	yŭsaccinu, yŭsacnu
fem. [saccana]	yŭsaccana, yŭsacna	yŭsaccina, yŭsacna
2. *masc.* [saccantunu]	tŭsaccanu, tŭsacnu	tŭsaccinu, tŭsacnu
fem. [saccantina]	tŭsaccana, tŭsacna	tŭsaccina, tŭsacna
1. ?	nŭsaccan	nŭsaccin
Dual. 3. [saccanā]	[yŭsaccanā]	[yŭsaccinā]

IMPERATIVE.	PRECATIVE.	INFINITIVE.	PARTICIPLE.
Sing. 2. *masc.* succin (sucin)	*Sing.* 3. lusaccan, lusaccin	saccanu	musaccinu˙
fem. succini	1. lusaccan		
Plu. 2. *masc.* succinu	*Plu.* 3. *masc.* lusaccanu	INFINITIVE PASSIVE.	
fem. succina	*fem.* lusaccana	succunu	

IPHTAEL.

PERMANSIVE (or Perfect).	PRESENT.	AORIST.
Not found.	*Sing.* 3. *masc.* yustaccan	yustaccin, yuptekid
	etc., etc.	etc., etc.

IMPERATIVE.	PRECATIVE.	INFINITIVE.	PARTICIPLE.
Not found.	*Sing.* 3. lustaccan	[sataccānu]	mustaccinu
	etc., etc.		

SHAPHEL.

PERMANSIVE (or Perfect).		PRESENT.	AORIST.
Not found.	*Sing.* 3. *masc.*	yŭsascan	yŭsascin, yŭsescin
	fem.	tŭsascan	tŭsascin, tŭsescin
	2. *masc.*	tŭsascan	tŭsascin, tŭsescin
	fem.	tusascani	tŭsascini, tŭsescini
	1.	'ūsascan	'ūsascin, 'ūsescin
	Plu. 3. *masc.*	yŭsascanu	yŭsascinu, yŭsescinu
	fem.	yŭsascana	yŭsascina, yŭsescina
	2. *masc.*	tŭsascanu	tŭsascinu, tŭsescinu
	fem.	tŭsascana	tŭsascina
	1.	nŭsascan	nŭsascin, nŭsescin
	Dual. 3.	[yŭsascanā]	[yŭsascinā]

IMPERATIVE.	PRECATIVE.	INFINITIVE.	PARTICIPLE.
Sing. 2. *masc.* suscin	*Sing.* 3. lusascan	sascānu	mŭsascinu
fem. suscini	1. lusascin		
Plu. 2. *masc.* suscinu	*Plu.* 3. *masc.* lusascinu	INFINITIVE PASSIVE.	
fem. suscina	*fem.* lusascina	suscunu	

ISTAPHAL.

PERMANSIVE (or Perfect).	PRESENT.	AORIST.
Not found.	*Sing.* 3. *masc.* yustascan *or* yultascan	yustascin *or* yultascin
	etc., etc.	etc., etc.

IMPERATIVE.	PRECATIVE.	INFINITIVE PASSIVE.	PARTICIPLE.
Sing. 2. *masc.* sutiscin	*Sing.* 3. lustascan	sutescunu	mustascinu
etc., etc.	etc., etc.		multascinu

THE CONJUGATIONS.

(1) KAL, *ictum* he concealed

(2) NIPHAL, *iccatum* (*incatum*) he was concealed

(3) PAEL, *yŭcattum* he did conceal

(4) SHAPHEL, *yŭsactum* he caused to conceal

(1*a*) IPHTEAL, *ictatum*

(1*b*) IPHTANEAL, *ictantum*

(2*a*) ITTAPHAL, *ittactum* (*intactum*)

(2*b*) ITTANAPHAL, *ittanacatum*

(3*a*) IPHTAEL, *yuctattum*

(3*b*) IPHTANAEL, *yuctanattum*

(4*a*) ISTAPHAL, *yustactum, yultactum*

(4*b*) ISTANAPHAL, *yustanactum*

(5) APHEL (in concave verbs), *yudhib*, he caused to be good

(5*a*) ITAPHAL, *yutadhib*

(2*c*) NIPHAEL, *iccattum*

(4*c*) SHAPHAEL, *yuscattum*

(3*d*) PAEL PASSIVE, *yucuttum* (Permansive   (4*d*) SHAPHEL PASSIVE, *yuscutum* (Permansive
      cuttum)   *sucutum* or *sucatum*)

(5*d*) APHEL PASSIVE, *yudhub*   (4*ad*) ISTAPHAL PASSIVE (Permansive), *sutactim*

(2*e*) NIPHALEL, *iccatumim*   (3*e*) PALEL, *yŭcattumim*

(4*e*) SHAPHALEL, *yŭsactumim*   (3*f*) IPHTATAEL, *yuctatatsir* he marshalled

(1*e*) PILEL, *iddanan* he gives   (4*f*) ISTATAPHEL, *yustetesir* he made straight

(1*g*) POEL, *ilubus* he put on   (1*ag*) IPHTOEL, *etupus* he made

A TIPHEL occurs in defective verbs like *tesub* (אשב), *tebusu* (עבש), *tebu* (בוא).

DEFECTIVE VERBS.

VERBS פ"ן.

	PERMANSIVE.	PRESENT.	AORIST.	IMPERATIVE.	PARTICIPLE.
Kal	namir *he sees*	inammir, inammar	immur, immar *he saw*	umur, amur	námiru *or*
			iddin *he gave*	idin	namru
			ippal *he threw down*	apal	
			ecil *he ate*	ecil	
Iphteal	nitmur	ittamar	ittamir	nitmir	muttamiru
Niphal	nammur	innamar	innamir	nammir	munnamiru
Ittaphal	[nattemur]	ittammar	ittammir	[nitammir]	muttamaru
Pael	nammar	yŭnammar	yŭnammir	nummir	munammiru
Iphtael	—	yuttammar	yuttammir	—	muttammiru
Shaphel	[sammar]	yŭsammar	yŭsammir	summir	musammiru
Istaphal	[satnemar]	yustammar	yustammir	suttimmir	mustammiru
Shaphael	[sanammar]	yusnammar	yusnammir	sunummir	musnammiru
Istaphael	—	yustenammar	yustenammir	—	mustenammiru
Pael Passive	nummur	yunummar	yunummir	—	—
Iphtael Passive	—	yuttummar	yuttummir	—	—
Shaphel Passive	{ sunumur / sunamur }	yusummar	yusummir	—	—
Istaphal Passive	sutenumur	yustummar	yustummir	—	—
Shaphael Passive	{ sunummur / sunammur }	yusnummar	yusnummir	—	—

VERBS פ״א.

	PERMANSIVE.	PRESENT.	AORIST.	IMPERATIVE.	PARTICIPLE.
Kal	asab	yasab	yasib, isib, ecul	esib, sib, acul, cul	asibu
Iphteal	tesub	itasab	itasib, itesib	itsib	mutasabu
Niphal	[nāsub]	inasab	inasib	nasib	munasibu
Ittaphal	—	ittesab	ittesib	—	muttesibu
Pael	[assab]	yussab	yussib	ussib	mussibu
Iphtael	—	yŭtassab	yŭtassib	[itasab]	mutassabu
Shaphel	[sāsab]	yŭsasab, yŭsesab	yŭsasib, yŭsesib	susib	musesibu
Istaphal	[satesab]	yustesab	yustesib	sutesib, sutesab	mustesibu
Istataphal	[satetesab]	[yustetesab]	yustetesib	[sutetesib]	[mustetesibu]
Itaphal	—	yutesab	yutesib	[utesib]	mutesibu
Pael Passive	ussub	yu'ussab	yu'ussub	—	—
Istaphal Passive	sutesub	[yustusab]	yustusib	—	—

VERBS פ״ה.

	PERMANSIVE.	PRESENT.	AORIST.	IMPERATIVE.	PARTICIPLE.
Kal	halac	ihabid *he destroys* illac (ihlac) *he goes*	ihbid, illic	halic	halicu, allicu
Iphteal	—	itallac	itallic	itlic	mŭtallacu
Niphal	[nalluc]	inallac	inallic	nallic	mŭnallicu
Ittaphal	—	ittallac	ittallic	—	muttallicu
Ittanaphal	—	ittanalac	ittanalic	—	muttanalicu
Pael	hallac	{ yu'allac / yuhabbad }	{ yu'allic / yuhabbid }	hullic	mu'allicu
Iphtael	—	yŭtallac	yŭtallic	[itallic]	mŭtallicu
Shaphel	[sallac]	yŭsallac	yŭsallic	sulic, sullic	musallicu
Istaphal	[satallac]	yustallac	yustallic	sutallic	mustallicu
Pael Passive	[hulluc]	[yu'ullac]	[yu'ullic]	—	—
Shaphel Passive	suluc	[yusullac]	[yusulluc]	—	—

VERBS פ״י.

	PERMANSIVE.	PRESENT.	AORIST.	IMPERATIVE.	PARTICIPLE.
Kal	ulid	yulad	yulid *he begat*	lid	alidu, ulidu
Iphteal	[telud]	itulad	itulid	—	mutelidu
Niphal	[nulud]	[inelad]	[inelid]	nulid	munelidu
Ittaphal	—	ittulad	ittulid	—	muttelidu
Pael	[ullad]	yu'ullad, yullad	yu'ullid, yullid	ullid	mullidu
Iphtael	—	yŭtullad	yŭtullid	—	muttelladu
Shaphel	[sulad]	yŭselad	yŭselid	sulid	musalidu
Istaphal	[sutelad]	yustelad	yustelid	sutelid	mustelidu

VERBS פ״י.

	PERMANSIVE.	PRESENT.	AORIST.	IMPERATIVE.	PARTICIPLE.
Kal	[inik]	inak	inik *he suckled*	nik	iniku
Iphteal	[tenuk]	itinak	itinik	itnik	mutiniku
Niphal	[nenuk]	ininak	ininik	ninik	muniniku
Ittaphal	—	ittinak	ittinik	[nitinik]	muteniku
Pael	[ennak]	innak, i'ennak	innik, i'ennik	unnik	mu'enniku
Iphtael	—	yuttennak	yuttennik	ittinnik	muttenniku
Shapel	[senak]	yusenak	yusenik	sunik	museniku
Istaphal	[satenak]	yustenak	yustenik	sutenik	musteniku
Istataphal	[satetinak]	yustetenak	yustetenik	[sutetenik]	[musteteniku]

VERBS פ״ע.

	PERMANSIVE.	PRESENT.	AORIST.	IMPERATIVE.	PARTICIPLE.
Kal	epis	epas *he makes*	epus, emid, e'ibus, ippus	epus	episu
Iphteal	etpus	etappas	etepus, etippis	etpis	mutepisu
Niphal	[nepus]	ippas, ipas	ippis, ipis	nippis, nipis	munepisu
Ittaphal	[netepus]	ittepas	ittepis	nitepis	mutepisu
Pael	[eppas]	yuppas	yuppis, yu'ubbis	uppis	muppisu
Iphtael	—	yŭteppas	yŭteppis	—	mutteppisu
Shaphel	[sepas]	yusepas	yusepis	supis	musepisu
Istaphal	[setepas]	yustepas	yustepis	suttepis	mustepisu
Hithpoel	—	[etupas]	etupus	—	—

CONCAVE VERBS ע״א, ע״ו, ע״י, ע״ע.

	PERMANSIVE.	PRESENT.	AORIST.	IMPERATIVE.	PARTICIPLE.
Kal	cain *he established*	itar *he brings back*	itur	tir, tar	ta'iru, ca'inu
	kâm *he raised*		iciś *he cut off*	duk *strike*	[Part. Pass. diku]
Iphteal	tebācu *I came*	itbā, ictan ittar	itbu', ictin imtut *he died*	[ictun] [tebu]	muctinu
Niphalel	[nacnun]	iccanan	iccanin, izzanun *it rained*	nacnin	muccaninu
Ittaphalel	[nactenun]	ittacnan	ittacnin	nitacnin	muttacnanu
Pael	ciyin, nikh *it rested*	yu'uccan, yuccan	yu'uccin, yuccin	[uccin]	muccinu
Iphtael	—	yuctan	yuctin	—	mutaccinu
Palel	cunnu *they established*	yucnan	yucnin	ucnin	mucninu

	PERMANSIVE.	PRESENT.	AORIST.	IMPERATIVE.	PARTICIPLE.
Iphtalel	—	ictenan	ictenin	—	—
Shaphel	[sacân]	yusacan	yusacin, yusacen	sucun	musaccinu
Istaphal	[satecan]	yustacan	yustacin, yustecin	sutcun	mustacinu
Aphel	—	yucayan	yucayin, yucin	cin, cun	mucinu
Itaphal	—	yuccan	yuccin	—	muccinu
Shaphael	[saccan]	yŭsaccan	yŭsaccin	succun	mŭsaccinu
Istaphael	[sateccan]	yustaccan	[yustaccin]	[suteccin]	mustaccinu
Shaphel Passive	sucun ⁻	yusucan	yusucin, yusucun	—	—

VERBS ל״ע, ל״י, ל״ו, ל״ה, ל״א.

	PERMANSIVE.	PRESENT.	AORIST.	IMPERATIVE.	PARTICIPLE.
Kal	nasu *he lifts up*, bane *he creates*	igabbi' *he speaks*, ilikku' *he takes*	ibnu', ikbi'	ban, bani, pit *open*, piti	banu
Iphteal	[kitbu']	ikteba¹	iktebi'	kitbi'	muktebū
Pael	[kabba']	yŭkabba'	yŭkabbi'	kubbi'	mukabbū
Iphtael	—	yuktabba'	yuktabbi'	kitibbi'	muktabbu
Niphal	nakbu'	ikkaba'	ikkabi	nakbi'	mukkabū
Ittaphal	[naktebu']	ittakba'	ittakbi'	nitakbi'	muttakbū
Niphael	[nakabbu']	ikkabba'	ikkabbi'	[nakabbi']	mukkabbū
Shaphel	[sakba']	yŭsakba'	yŭsakbi'	sukbu'	mŭsakbū
Istaphal	[satkeba']	yustekba'	yustekbi'	sutekbi'	mustekbū
Shaphael	[sakabba']	yuskabba'	yuskabbi'	sukubbu'	muskabbū
Istaphael	[satkabba']	yustekabba'	yustekabbi'	[sutekabbi']	mustekabbū
Pael Passive	kubbu'	yukubba'	yukubbu'	—	—
Shaphael Passive	sukubu', sukbu'	yuskubba'	yuskubbi'	—	—

QUADRILITERALS.

	PERMANSIVE.	PRESENT.	AORIST.	IMPERATIVE.	PARTICIPLE.
Kal	palcit *he crossed*	ipalcat, iśkhupar *he overthrows*	ipalcit, iplacit, iparassid *he pursues*	palcit	mŭpalcitu
Iphtalel	[pitlucut]	yuptalcat	yuptalcit	pitalcat	muptalcitu
Shaphalel	[saplacat]	yuspalcat	yuspalcit	supalcut	mŭpalcitu
Istaphalel	[saptelcat]	yustapalcat	yustapalcit	sitpalcut	mustapalcitu
Niphalel	[naplacut]	ippalcat	ippalcit, ippalaccit, ipparsud *he pursued*	nipalcat	muppalcitu
Ittaphalel	[naptelcut]	ittapalcat	ittapalcit	[natepalcat]	muttapalcitu
Niphalella	—	ippalcatat	ippalcitit	—	muppalcittu

9

LECTURE VIII.

Assyrian Syntax.

———

SYNTAX, or the arrangement of words in a sentence, introduces us to fully-formed speech. The more developed a language is, the richer and more delicate will its syntax be. English, which has so largely shaken off the trammels of flexion and the cumbrous grammatical inheritance of a half-barbarous age, has a peculiarly elaborate syntax; syntactical construction, in fact, has taken the place in it of accidence. The relations of the sentence, which were once denoted by special terminations, are now expressd by means of the position and order of words. On the other hand, wherever a language has carried composition to an excess, as is the case with Sanskrit, the syntax will suffer correspondingly.

Now the syntax of the Semitic languages is comparatively simple. The relations of the different parts of the sentence to one another, as well as of one sentence to another, are almost childish in their simplicity. We shall look in vain for that rich array of conjunctive particles such as we find in Greek, or for the manifold shades of meaning that can be expressed in our own tongue by words like "when," "as," or "but." The Semite has hardly risen above the primitive mode of marking a subordinate sentence by placing it side by side with the principal one; the various kinds of subordinate clauses and the different ideas they convey to us are all introduced by a single monotonous "and." The individual sentence itself offers little complexity or variety; composition and abstracts are rare, and the order of words is more or less fixed. Assyrian syntax shares all the characteristics of the syntax of the cognate dialects; indeed it is somewhat simpler and more primitive than that of either Hebrew or Arabic. There is a sameness and monotony about it which is almost wearying, and the number of rules to which it conforms is limited and uniform.

Let us first consider the syntax of the single sentence, and then pass on to that of a sentence which stands in relation to another.

The simplest form of sentence is that which consists of subject and predicate connected together by the copula. In this case the predicate is an attribute of the subject, but conceived of not as an attribute which necessarily forms part of the idea of the subject, but asserted of the subject as something additional to the idea previously formed of it. The expression "the good king" is a single whole, the statement "the king is good" is a judgment which presupposes reflection and comparison. In short, wherever we have subject and predicate, there we have comparison and analysis, the act of comparison being denoted by the logical copula. Where we have merely subject and attribute, that is to say substantive and adjective, we have synthesis rather than analysis. Assyrian, however, made no outward distinction between the two kinds of attribution. *Ilu rabu* might mean either "the great god" or "the god is great;" the context alone can decide. We find no "verb" to express the logical copula, nor do we find any use of the personal pronoun with a preposition in the place of the substantive verb, such as is common in the allied Semitic dialects. The only mode by which the predicate could be pointed out was by employing a substantive to express it, and so setting two substantives side by side without any intervening verb or particle. As a general rule, the predicate preceded its subject, as in the cognate tongues, unless special emphasis were to be laid upon it. Thus we have *ilu rabu Akhurmazdah* "Ormazd (is) a great god," *ul assati atta* (for *atti*) "thou (art) not my wife,"[1] but *anacu Khisi'arsah* "I (am) Xerxes."

The predicate, however, might be represented by a verb as well as by an adjective or a substantive. We have already seen that in the Semitic languages the verb presupposes the noun, and that the Assyrian aorist and permansive are merely combinations of nouns with the personal pronouns. If *existence*, pure and simple, had to be expressed, the Assyrians made use of *basu*, a verb which is derived from the combination of a preposition *ba* with the

---

[1] *W. A. I.* II., 10, 10.

pronoun *su*, like the Ethiopic *bô*, by Dr. Schrader and Prof. Wright.[1] By the side of the positive *basu* stood the negative *yânu* "not to be," the equivalent of the Hebrew אֵין. *Possession* was denoted by *isu* "to have," the Hebrew יֵשׁ, and other attributive ideas were expressed in the same way. *'Sarru icassid*, for instance, may be translated either "the king conquers" or "the king is a conqueror."

We will now turn back to the synthetic use of the attribute, when along with the substantive to which it is attached it forms part of a single concept which would be incomplete without it. The synthetic use of the attribute is logically later than its analytic use, since we cannot call a king "good," for example, until we have come to the conclusion, or formed the judgment, that he is so. When employed synthetically, the attribute may be either an adjective or the genitive of a substantive. So far as meaning is concerned, there is no difference between "a ring of gold" and "a golden ring." In Assyrian, when the attribute was an adjective, it had to agree in gender, number and case with its substantive, that is to say, the grammatical terminations of the two nouns were required to be the same. Thus we should have *sarru rabu* "the great king," but *sarri rabi* "great kings." Of course where different terminations were employed with the same grammatical signification, the adjective might adopt one and the substantive another; we might say, for example, *sarrani rabi* as well as *sarri rabi*. The decay of the case-endings caused a further violation of the general rule. Hence we come across such anomalies as *libba cinu* "a fixed heart," *garri-ya makhra* "my former campaign." The decay which attacked the case-endings, however, tended to spread to the other indices of flexion as well. Now and then in the later inscriptions we find a masculine adjective joined with a feminine substantive, or *vice versâ*, and even a singular put in the place of a plural. Thus in the inscriptions of the Persian period we read *irtsitiv aga* "this earth," although here it would seem that *agā* is used as an indeclinable and consequently genderless word. But as early as the time of Tiglath-Pileser I.[2] we get *musarripa* "enflaming" as an epithet of *Istar* and *bilitu*, unless, indeed, we are to read *musarripah* and consider the word as an example of the softening

---

[1] For my own part I prefer Oppert's comparison with the Ethiopic *bisi* "men," as I find no traces of a preposition *ba* in Assyrian.

W. A. I. I., 9, 14.

of the final *at* into *ah*. The verbs, however, show that a sense of the distinction between the terminations of the masculine and feminine had become weakened as far back as the twelfth century B.C. Tiglath-Pileser I. says of "the great gods" *ili rabi*, who are, of course, masculine, *aga'a tsira tuppira-su* "the supreme crown ye have entrusted to him," where the verb is feminine; though, it is true, we might explain the form *tuppira* here as belonging to the objective aorist, and so standing for *tuppiru'a* (*tuppiruna*). But the frequent use of a feminine nominative with a third person masculine in the later days of the Assyrian empire favours the first view. Assur-bani-pal tells us that "Istar," *ana ummani-ya sutta yusapri-va ciham icbi-sunut*, "to my soldiers a dream disclosed and thus declared unto them" (Sm. *A.*, 221, 23), and in the "Descent of Istar into Hades" (I. 3) we have *Istar banat 'Sini uzun-sa . . . . iscun*·"Istar, the daughter of the moon-god, set her ear."[1] In the Assyrian translation of the famous tablet of ancient Accadian laws (*W. A. I.* II., 10) there is a very curious neglect of the genders, the masculine being used for the feminine not only in the case of the verbs (as *ictabi* for *tactabi*), but even in that of the pronouns (as *atta* for *atti* and *su* for *sa* or *si*) ; but the explanation of this must be sought in the fact that the translation was probably made by a scribe of Accadian origin, who had not been accustomed to distinguish the two genders from each other. *Nisi* "men," however, in the abstract sense of "humanity," is sometimes used with a feminine adjective, as in *W. A. I.* III., 41, 39, where we find *nisi disâti* "abandoned men," just as in the Behistun inscription (line 16) *ukum* "people" is joined with the plural *gabbi* "all," and *itticru'* "they revolted." The want of agreement in number is much rarer than that in gender, and occurs only with nouns used in a collective sense, or where the adjective is more or less independent of its substantive. Thus we not unfrequently find the expression *sarri alic makhriya* (*W. A. I.* II., 21, 29) "the kings who went before me," where the full force of the words would be "the kings, each goer before me." The decay of the dual naturally caused it to be generally construed with a plural predicate.

The attribute, we have seen, may be the genitive of a second substantive as well as an adjective. The genitive-ending of a large class of Sanskrit and

---

[1] Compare, too, in the Babylonian transcription of the Naksh-i-Rustam inscription (9, 10), the use of the feminine *matati* "countries," with the masculine *inassunu* "will bring," which is similarly found with the masculine *itturunu* "they have returned" at Behistun (7).

classical nouns was originally adjectival, the Greek δημοῦ, for instance, which stands for an earlier δημόσιο (Sansk. -asya), being formed by the adjectival suffix *tya*, and so differing but little from δημόσιος. Like the attributive adjective, the attributive genitive followed its substantive in the Semitic languages, and the two words were as closely combined in pronunciation as they were in sense. They were in fact pronounced in one breath, an external symbol of the fact that they together made up but one idea. As we have seen in a former Lecture the first or governing noun lost its case-endings in Assyrian when in the "construct state," so that "the house of the king" would be *bit sarri* instead of *bitu sarri*. Originally the attributive noun took the light genitive ending in -*i*, which was a weakening of the termination of the objective case (-*a*), just as the genitive relation itself was a weakened form of the objective relation. Two substantives might follow one another, each in the construct state, as in the other Semitic languages; thus we get *Nabu pákid cissat same u irtsitiv* "Nebo, the overseer of the hosts of heaven and earth" (*W. A. I.* I., 51, 1, 13). As also in the other Semitic languages, however, the possessive pronoun suffix might be regarded as an adjective, and attached to the second member of a genitival compound without causing the latter to lose its case-endings. *Unut takhazi-sunu*, for example, is "their munition of war" (Lay. 16, 46), *nisi takhazi-ya* "my men of war" (*W. A. I.* I., 39, 44). A violation of the rule by which the governing noun lost its case-endings is a very rare occurrence, and is usually capable of explanation. Sometimes the nouns are in apposition one to another, and not in the genitive relation, as in such a phrase as *belutu Assur* "the lordship of Assyria" (properly "the lordship, that is Assyria"), or *pulkhu melam Assuri* "fear, even the onset of Assyria," that is, "the fearful onset of Assyria."[1] Sometimes the first noun is plural, and the final vowel is consequently a mark not of case but of number, as in *rabbi biti* "chiefs of the house." Sometimes the anomaly is due to the fact that the first noun forms part of a compound preposition, like *ina tuculti* "in the service of," *ina libbi* "in the midst of," where the analogy of the other prepositions *itti* "with," *arci* "after," *eli* "above," *adi* "up to," etc. (like the Heb. עֲלִי, עֲדִי, etc.) has been followed. One of the few real exceptions to the ordinary rule is to be discovered in *W. A. I.* II., 66, 4, where Beltis is called *bucurti Anuv* "the eldest-born of Anu," instead of the

---

[1] *Melam* I derive from the root לוה.

more correct *bucrat*. In fact, so far as I know, the only cases in which the rule is broken are where the feminine ending *-ăti* with two short vowels follows a preceding short vowel.

I must here turn aside for a moment to notice an apparently converse anomaly that occasionally presents itself in the texts, where a noun, though not in the construct state, seems to be without the case-endings. The anomaly, however, is apparent only, and arises from the deficiencies of the Assyrian mode of writing. The last root-syllable of a word, if it begins and ends with a consonant, may be expressed by a single character; in this case the short vowel of the case is not added but left to be supplied by the reader. Thus *kakkadu* " head " may be written ⯮ ⯮, where we must read not *kak-kad* but *kak-kadu; panu limnu* " evil face," ⯬⯭ ⯬⯭ ⯯, where the first ideograph must be sounded *panu* and not *pan*.

Nowhere can the attributive sense of the genitive relation be seen more clearly than in the way in which abstracts were frequently represented in Assyrian as in the cognate languages. This was by combining a substantive expressing the possessor or subject with another substantive expressing the attribute, so that *bel-khidhdhi* " the lord of sin " would mean " a rebel " (*W. A. I.* I., 37, 39), *nis rucubi* " the man of chariots," " the charioteers," and *er sarruti-su* " the city of his royalty," " his royal city." So close is the combination that when the plural is required the sign of it may be attached to the second substantive only, while a negative sense may be obtained by prefixing the negative particle, as in *la-bel-cussu* " the not-lord-of-the-throne," that is " an usurper." We all remember similar modes of expression in the Bible, where " the daughter of Zion " signifies " the inhabitants of Jerusalem," and the New Testament writer uses " the son of peace " instead of the abstract " peace," in imitation of the Hebrew idiom.

As in the other Semitic languages, so, too, in Assyrian the construct state came in later times to be replaced by an analytical periphrasis. The synthesis between the two parts of the idea, the subject and its attribute, was broken up, and a construction adopted which involved an assertion of judgment. In other words, the predicate took the place of the attribute. This was effected by placing the demonstrative *sa* " that," which in course of time assumed a relative signification, between the substantive and its attributive genitive. *'Sarru sa Assur* " the king, that (is) Assyria " was substituted for the simpler *sar Assur* " Assyria's king," and so the pronoun *sa* came gradually to have the force of our preposition " of." The analytical character of this construction can best be observed where the predicate precedes the subject, as in *sa sanati arkhi* " of the year the months " (*W. A. I.* III., 52, 43), though in such instances the second noun ought to have the possessive pronoun suffix, as *insa Cambuziya aga-su akhu-su* " of Cambyses this man his brother," a construction permissible in Ethiopic, but rarely found in Arabic and later Hebrew. In some cases the introductory *sa* would be most idiomatically rendered by " as to " or " regarding " (e.g., *sa Ambarissi malic-sunu* " as regards Ambaris their king "), and we even find instances in which it is dropped altogether.

The periphrastic genitive served to express the superlative as in the phrase *Akhuramazda rabu sa ili*, " Ormazd, the greatest of the gods."

The predicative relation constitutes the germ of the sentence. But the sentence does not become complete until it possesses an object. A subject implies an object as much as it implies a predicate, and a predicate can only be made definite and concrete by being provided with an object. " The king is a conqueror " is a merely general statement; it becomes definite by the addition of the object he has conquered. Predicative sentences have little practical utility; the assertion that " man is mortal " may be very fitting for works on logic, but it would not be of the slightest assistance towards supplying us with the needs of our every-day life. The first speakers must have contented themselves with objective sentences, and left predicative sentences to their more intellectual descendants. Indeed, since the satisfaction of his wants must have been the primary motive in primitive man for the creation of language, the indication of the object would have been of supreme importance to him, and accordingly we find in all languages that the objective case is older than the subjective.

Now an objective sentence is one in which the action passes on from the subject to the object; where, therefore, the two factors are contrasted together in the mind as independent but related. The object is conceived as essentially distinct from the subject, unlike the predicate which is conceived as forming part of it. The most natural way of contrasting the subject and the object would consist in their immediate juxtaposition, and the primitive savage who said, " Me, pear ! " would be quite as intelligible as the Englishman of to-day who says, " I want a pear." We find children constantly returning to this primitive method of expression. If the subject and object are thus contrasted by being placed side by side, the verb or representative of action will have to follow the object, that is will come at the end of the sentence. And such we find to be the case with barbarous languages which have arrived at the conception of a verb, as well as with more cultured ones which have retained their original usage. This, too, is the order of the ideas and words in a sentence adopted by the deaf and dumb. In course of time, however, the natural order is likely to be replaced by the logical order, according to which the object will follow the verb or representative of action. That to which the action passes, and where, therefore, it finds its rest and fulfilment, is logically last.

Unlike Hebrew, Assyrian observes the natural order of words in the sentence rather than the logical one. The Assyrian verb regularly comes at the end of a clause. The chief exception is when the objective form of the tenses is used, and here, in unconscious remembrance, it would seem, of the time when the objective aorist and present were merely verbal nouns, the verb precedes the case it governs. The personal pronouns, again, are affixed to the verbal forms, but this is due to the fact that the verbal forms were once nouns, to which the possessive pronouns were attached according to rule. When the possessive form of the pronoun is not used, the pronoun precedes the verb like other words; thus we have in the inscriptions of the Persian period: *Urimizda sarrutav anacu iddannu* (*idánu*) " Ormazd has given me the sovereignty" (Beh. 24), *mandattuv anacu inassunu* "they will bring me the tribute " (Naksh-i-Rustam, 9, 10), *anacu Akhurmazdah litstsurá-ni* " as for me, may Ormazd protect me." The last example but one shows that the verb may have two objects, the remoter object or dative standing after the nearer object or accusative. The dative of the pronoun, however, is generally expressed by the suffixed possessive; e.g., *sane cráni dannuti* . . . *addin-su* " two strong cities I gave him " (Khors. 52), xxii. *biráti iddin-su* " twenty-two fortresses he gave him " (Khors. 39). In this Assyrian agrees with Hebrew and Ethiopic. Where the dative is not a pronoun, however, the preposition *ana* is employed, as in *dunku ana nisi iddínu* " he has given prosperity to men " (N.-R. 2), the compound *ana eli* being used with a pronoun (as *ana eli-su idricuh* " they pursued after him " Beh. 16). In the later dialect of the Achæmenian inscriptions, when Aramaisms had penetrated into the language, the same preposition *ana* is used like the Aramaic ־ל to denote the accusative, which then mostly follows the verb. Thus we read (*aducu*) *ana Gumātav* " (I had killed) Gomates " (Beh. 109), *sa ana khisi'arsah sarra ibnu* "who has made Xerxes king."[1] This use of *ana* is never met with in the inscriptions of Nineveh and Babylonia, and characterises the Achæmenian period.

The object of a sentence may be implicitly contained in the predicate or verb, and will then be expressed by a noun formed from the same root as the verb, and possessing a similar signification. Assyrian is particularly fond of this construction with "an accusative of cognate meaning," as the grammarians term it, and numberless examples might be collected from the inscriptions. Thus we meet with such phrases as *acul acalu* "I ate food continuously," *dicta-sun aduc* "their slayables (soldiers) I slew" (*W. A. I.* II., 67, 9), *khirit-su akhri* "its ditch I dug," *ikhtanabbata khubut nisi sa Assur* "he is ever wasting the wasting of the men of Assyria" (Sm. *A.*, 258, 113). The use of the infinitive absolute in Hebrew is not dissimilar; like the Assyrian construction, it expresses the ideas of intensity and continuation which naturally arise from the specification of the exact object of the predicate. In Hebrew (and Ethiopic) the infinitive absolute stands after the verb when continuance is denoted, before it when intensity is implied. In Syriac also it stands before the verb when the idea of intensity is to be marked, whereas Arabic requires the converse position in such a case. It will be seen that Assyrian in this respect agrees with Hebrew, and the usage seems to go back to very ancient date. Continuous action is naturally expressed by setting the object after the verb, while attention would be drawn to the intensive character of an action by placing the object of it in the foreground. The Arabic usage is probably of later growth than that of Hebrew or Assyrian. The Assyrian "accusative of cognate meaning" is sometimes accompanied by the preposition *ana*, like the Hebrew infinitive with ־ל; e.g., *batuli-sun va batulāte-sun ana sagaltu asgul* "their boys and maidens I dishonoured." Still more analogous to the Hebrew construction are such expressions as *anacu dhēmu altacan ana sadhari limsu* "I gave orders to write an inscription,"[2] *ana epis ramani-su* "to the working of himself," where *sadhari* and *epis* are infinitives, the latter in the construct state, the former preserving its verbal force, and so retaining its

---

[1] Inscription at Elwend, lines 9, 10.   [2] Inscription at Van, line 7.

case-termination. These instances will explain the use of the infinitive with the negative, as in *adi la basē* "up to the not being" (i.e. "till there were no more "),[1] *ina la bana* "in the not-doing" (i.e. "while I had leisure "), *ana la casad-i ina mati-su* "for the not getting of me (in order that I might not get) to his country" (*W. A. I.* I., 10, 45).

The subject may be understood or implied in the verb, or it may be expressed by a pronoun. Thus the third person plural may be used impersonally, as in the curious phrase *kharsānu sakūtu epis buhri-sunu ikbi'uni-su* "it had been ordered him to make snares in the high woods" (literally "the high woods (for) the making of their snares they had appointed unto him "),[2] or it may express the indeterminate third person, as when we read *ana mat Nizir sa mat Lullu-linipa ikabu-su-ni akdhirib* "to the country of Nizir, which they call the country of Lullu-linipa, I drew near" (*W. A. I.* I., 20, 34) ; and in a conditional sentence *lū ana ziga yusetstsu'u* "or should anyone expose to harm" (*W. A. I.* I., 70, 11). The third person singular is frequently used in the same way, and so we have *illica* "one came," *yusapri* "one revealed." These impersonal singulars often take the place of the passive. A subject is occasionally supplied in the shape of *nisu* "man," used in a collective sense, as, for instance, *nisu sa mat 'Sukhi ana mat Assuri la illicūni* "none of the Nomad Arabs had gone to Assyria." This employment of *nisu* as a subject is parallel with the employment of the third personal pronouns as objects. They could be employed in the same indefinite way as that in which we sometimes employ "it," in order to sum up collectively all that has gone before. *Ana bit cili la isarrac-si* means "to the store-house he does not deliver them" (*W. A. I.* I., 27, 36) ; where the feminine singular *si* refers to the columns and other palace-decorations which had been spoken of before. The masculine singular may sometimes be translated "people," as in *usalvi-s* "I caused the people to approach," or *usalic-su* "I caused the people to go ;" where a variant reading has the plural *sunu*. So, too, in accordance with the Semitic idiom which allowed a pronoun to be added pleonastically at the end of a sentence, we read *sallut-su va camut-su ana er-ya Asur ubla-su* "his spoils and his treasures to my city Assur I brought it" *W. A. I.* I., 13, 24) ; *unut takhazi-sunu ecim-su* "their materials of war I took it" (Lay. 90, 65).

As in the cognate languages, Assyrian verbs which denote such ideas as

---

[1] In the Inscription of Sennacherib published by Grotefend, line 31.   *W. A. I.* I., 28, 13.

those of *filling*, *giving*, *finding*, and the like, may take two accusatives, that is
to say two objects one nearer and the other more remote.   Thus "Assur,"
Rimmon-nirari declares, *malcut lasanan yumallu'u katá-su* "(with) the kingdom
of Lasanan has filled his hand;"[1] and elsewhere we have *dahtu imkhar-sunuti*
"the gift he received them" (*W. A. I.* I., 41, 28); *sa itstsuru mubar-su la ibah*
"which a bird (for) its crossing finds not" (*W. A. I.* I., 33, 48, 49); *sa masac
Ili-biahdi khammahi israpu* "who had burned the skin of Ili-biahdi with
heat" (*W. A. I.* I., 36, 25); an instance of the common employment of two
accusatives where one expresses an idea cognate with that of the verb.   Of
course transitive verbs in Shaphel and Shaphael take two accusatives, while
intransitive verbs may be followed by an accusative of similar meaning, like
illica urukh mūti "he went the path of death."   Here the object which is
implicitly contained in the predicate is definitely expressed, so that such
accusatives may be said to resemble the use of the definite article with the
noun.   A similar explanation must be given of the so-called accusatives of
direction which may follow a verb of motion; in *illicu ritsut-su* "they went to
his help," for instance, the object is that towards which the action travels and
in which it finds repose.

Now that we have considered the various relations in which the subject
and the object may stand to the verb, it is time to see what modifications the
verb itself, or rather the action it represents, may undergo.   In the first place
the action may be a compound one, consisting, that is to say, of two ideas.
Instances in which such a compound action is expressed by setting two verbs
side by side without a conjunction, are to be found in Assyrian, as in the
cognate tongues.   Thus *irdu'u illicu kakkar tsummi* "they descended, they
went to dry ground," means "they went down to dry ground," where the
force of the English adverb is represented by a second verb.   In the second
place the action may be modified temporally, the time at which it took place
or the relation in which it stood to the subject or object being regarded
differently.   To meet such modifications various tenses are used, and Assyrian,
as we have seen when dealing with the verb, was, for a Semitic language,
peculiarly rich in tenses.   It is needless here to repeat what has been already
stated in regard to these tenses; it must be clear by this time what was the
force and use of the aorist, the present, the future, and the permansive, as

[1] *W. A. I.* I., 35, 3, 4.

well as of the subjective and objective aorists. It may be noted, however, that, as in Greek, the aorist was employed as an iterative present in similes and comparisons, what happens at any time being conceived to have already taken place on some definite occasion, as in *cima Rammanu izgum* "as the Air-god pours." The present, again, may be used instead of the future, whenever a future event is regarded as being so certain as to seem actually present, and the imperative is also found in the same sense. Finally in the third place the action may be regarded modally, that is to say, according to the manner in which it is regarded by the speaker as happening or likely to happen. From this point of view the sentence will be capable of a variety of modifications. I shall here pass over the moods that have been mentioned in the account of the conjugation, and confine myself to those different kinds of sentences which arise from the different ways or modes in which the action and its representative, the verb, may be looked at.

(1) The affirmative sentence simply states a fact, and as it has been abundantly illustrated by the examples previously given, I shall pass on to

(2) The negative sentence, formed by the two negative particles *la* and *ul*. The Hebrew distinction between לֹא and אַל, the first being used objectively and the second subjectively, has been lost in Assyrian, and in the place of it we find another distinction, according to which, while *la* is employed preferably with nouns, *ul* is employed with verbs. In the Achæmenian period of the language, however, *ul* came to be used with nouns as well as verbs, and Dr. Schrader may be right in thinking that *ul* was considered more emphatic than *la*. As the negative is really part of the idea expressed by the predicate, it does not require to be represented by a separate word, and Assyrian, accordingly, possessed a negative verb *yānu*, the Hebrew אִין. The primitive substantival character of *yānu* is illustrated by its use with the pronouns; *yānu-a*, for instance, literally "my not-being" is "I am not."

(3) Deprecatory sentences are formed by the help of the particle *ai*, the Ethiopic *'i*, Heb. אִ; thus *ai ipparcu'u idā-sa* "may its defences (*dual*) not be broken" (Lay. 42, 53), *ai isi naciri mugalliti* "may I not have enemies multiplied" (*W. A. I.* I., 58, 10, 15). In composition with the indefinite *umma* at the beginning of a clause, and with *ul* or *la* following immediately before the verb, *ai* signifies "no one whatsoever," as *aiumma ina libbi-sunu asar-su ul yumassi'i* "no one among them touched its site" (*W. A..I.* I.,

36, 36). Hence as the force of the negative lies in the second particle *ul* or *la*, *aiumma* came to have a purely indefinite sense when used by itself, and we may therefore translate it " any one whatever."

(4) A question is rarely found in the texts, and when it occurs has no such indicative particle as is possessed by Hebrew. In one of the bilingual hymns (*K.* 2861) we read: *ina same mannu tsīru* " in heaven who (is) supreme ? " *ina irtsitiv mannu tsīru* " in earth who (is) supreme ? " and at Naksh-i-Rustam (25): *matat annitav acca ikilsah* " those lands, how different are they ? "

(5) An intensive sentence may be indicated by the particle *lū* " verily " placed before the verb, though we also find it attached to a noun, as *anacu lū šarru* " I (am) indeed king " (*W. A. I.* I., 58, 9, 62). This use of *lū* led to its being employed as a mark of past time, like *kad* in Arabic, so that *lū allic* means " I went " (at a particular moment), *lūsardi*, for *lū usardi*, " I caused to add." Other modes of denoting an intensive sentence have already been noticed.

It would be needless to say more regarding (6) hortative and (7) precative sentences than that they are expressed by the imperative and precative moods. The " Descent of Istar " (5, 10) has preserved for us the interjection *allu* " woe ! " the Heb. אֲלָלַי.

The simple sentence sufficed for all the wants of primitive man. But with the growth of his intelligence and knowledge a combination of two or more sentences with one another came to be necessary. At first these were merely set side by side; then the relation of subordination which one of them implicitly bore to the other was made explicit by some external sign. Conjunctive and other particles came into use, the relative pronoun was developed, and the verbal forms underwent many modifications. The more advanced a language and the intellectual powers of its speakers, the more complicated become the relations of sentences to each other. Greek and English are good examples of the manifold ways in which one idea may be subordinated or related to another, and these relations represented by phonetic means. Assyrian, like the other Semitic tongues, was very much behind Greek or English in this respect. The compound sentence remained to the last comparatively simple, and the stock of modifying particles was not large.

The first mode adopted for connecting two sentences together was by employing the conjunction *va* "and," which in many languages, at all events, originally signified "further" or "addition." That this must once have been its meaning in Semitic also seems clear from the peculiar Assyrian habit of commencing a sentence with the verb and inserting the copulative conjunction between the verb and its subject, a habit, however, which becomes more frequent the older the inscriptions are. Thus in the account of the Deluge the Chaldean Noah says *usetsi-va summata* "I sent forth also a dove" (*W. A. I.* IV., 50, 38). Here the conjunction must be rendered "also" or "moreover." This half consciousness of its primitive signification will explain how the copulative conjunction "and" comes to be used as a separative "or," and an adversative "but." As in Hebrew, the conjunction *vā* or *ū* was weakened into an enclitic with a short vowel (*vă*) when employed with verbs, but whereas the Hebrew enclitic is prefixed to the word following, the Assyrian conjunction is postfixed to the verb (or verbal idea) that goes before. In this case it might even be contracted into a simple *-ă*. But the Assyrian *vă* did not possess the flexibility of the Hebrew ן, and the only trace of the use of *waw consecutivum* is to be found in sentences in which a subjective aorist is followed by a construct aorist or a permansive. Such sentences, however, are common enough in the inscriptions, and may be termed conditional. Thus we have *itsbatūni-vă emuru* "when they had taken they saw," *itsbatūni-vă tebuni* "when they had taken they came." Dr. Schrader remarks that the use of *waw* to express a circumstantial sentence seems unknown to Assyrian, where the present participle is preferred for the purpose; e.g., *ina er Cugunacca ina Parśu ásib su ina Elamti itbā* (Beh. 41) "in the city of Cugunacca in Parthia dwelling, into Elam he came."

A conditional sentence may be denoted by other means than the use of the enclitic *vă* with the subjective aorist. The particle *ci* is especially employed for this object, and it may be used with either the future, the subjective aorist, or the objective aorist. In the latter case, the objective aorist becomes a true subjunctive. Thus we find *ci ecalu ilabbiru-vă inakhu* "when the palace shall grow old and decay," *ci takabbu'u umma* "if thou shalt say thus" (N. R. 25), where the certainty of the event looked forward to is intended to be brought into relief. It is remarkable that Assyrian alone of the Semitic idioms should have developed the conditional sense of *cī;* in its use of *ci* as a particle of time it agrees with the cognate tongues. But *ci* was not the only particle which could be employed conditionally; besides *im* "if," *sa* is occasionally met with in the same sense, e.g., *sa lā agru'u-su igra-ni* " as I did not make war upon him he made war upon me." The subjunctive enclitic *-ni*, however, could be used by itself to express a condition, without any conditional particle going before; *yutsu-ni ner-ya itsbut*, for instance, must be rendered " when he came out he took my yoke." Here it will be seen that the conditional sense is almost absorbed by the temporal; this is not the case with the sentence *ikhkhara abdhu amattu sa pi-su yustenna* " (whoever) evades the pledge, the truth of his mouth changes" (*W. A. I.* I., 27, 86), where all indication of the condition is omitted.

Next to the simple copulative sentence, with the conditional that has grown out of it, will come the relative, which plays a considerable part in Assyrian syntax. The relative was originally a demonstrative, as our own use of *that* still shows, and such an expression as " he is the man whom I saw " would once have run " he is the man; that (man) I saw." The mere juxtaposition of the two clauses was sufficient to evolve the fact that the second was subordinate to the first, and in course of time the connecting link between the two, the demonstrative pronoun, acquired a meaning which expressed this subordination. In the periphrastic genitive, the Assyrian relative *sa*, which primarily denoted that the second noun belonged to a new sentence dependent upon the first, was crystallised into a mere sign of a case; elsewhere, however, it better preserved its integrity.

Instances of the ordinary construction of the relative may be found in almost every inscription of any length. In agreement, however, with the cognate languages, Assyrian preferred to make the reference to the antecedent clearer by attaching to the noun or verb which followed the relative the possessive or personal pronoun: thus *Yahudu sa asar-su ru'ku* " Judah whose place (is) remote," literally " of which its place (is) remote " (Lay. 33, 8); *sa ina abli-su* " upon whose son," literally " whom upon his son " (*W. A. I.* I., 35, 3, 2). This repetition of the pronoun, like the repetition of the negative, characterises a primitive state of speech when the understanding is less exercised, and accordingly requires language to be more definite and emphatic. The demonstrative (that is to say, the relative) is not at first felt to represent fully enough the idea which has gone before. Indeed the demonstrative was to some extent pleonastic; there was a time, as we have seen, when the mere juxtaposition of two sentences was sufficient to express the relation between them. Traces of this time survived in Assyrian, as in Hebrew poetry (and in our own language), in which the relative might be omitted; e.g., *itti kari ab-i iczuru* "with the castle my father had made" (*W. A. I.* I., 55, 5, 30), *assu khultuv ebusu* "on account of the wickedness he had done," *asar tallaci* "the place (to which) thou goest" (Sm. *A.*, 125, 61), *yumu annitu emuru* "the day he had seen that (dream)" (Sm. *A.*, 74, 19). The use of the indefinite *mannu* without *sa* is similar; thus *mannu atta sarru* "whatsoever king thou (mayest be)."

The relative may refer either to the whole of the preceding sentence (or idea) or to only part of it. It may, for instance, relate solely to a possessive pronoun suffix; of this we have an example at Naksh-i-Rustam (26), *tsalmaná-sunu amuru sa cússu attu-a nasu'u* "behold the images of those who uphold my throne." On the other hand it may refer to an unexpressed antecedent, and so be used substantivally, like our "what;" *ana sa ebúsu* is "what I have done," where the preposition is the sign of the accusative, *sa anacu ebus* "all that I did." This will explain the omission of the antecedent in the phrase *ina sa Gargamis* "according to the (maneh) of Carchemish," which would be literally "according to that which (is) of Carchemish" (*W. A. I.* III., 47, 9, 1).

This quasi-substantival employment of the relative led to its absolute use at the beginning of a clause, where it summed up all that had gone before. Thus we have *sa ana natsir citte va misari-su .... inambu-inni ili rabi* "as regards which, for the protection of its institutions and laws .... the great gods proclaim me" (*W. A. I.* I., 36, 40). Hence comes its adverbial use, as when we read *sa ... ina cussi sarruti rabis usibu* "when on my royal throne mightily I had sat" (*W. A. I.* I., 18, 44), where the temporal sense of the passage would ordinarily have required *ci*. It is remarkable that whereas *ci* is rarely used in this way in the other Semitic languages, Ethiopic exclusively, and Hebrew usually, apply it to the expression of statements of fact which are uniformly introduced by *sa* in Assyrian. Thus we get *sa Parsai ru'uku ultu mati-su tsaltav itebus* "(when wilt thou recognize) that the Persian far from his country made war" (N. R. 29), *sa la Barziya anacu* "that I (am) not Bardes" (Beh. 21). Dr. Schrader observes that after verbs which relate to the senses

a statement of fact is represented in Assyrian by a *nomen mutati* or infinitive ;
thus it is said of Merodach-Baladan that *halac girri-ya isme* "he heard of the
marching of my expedition," where in any other of the Semitic idioms we
should have had a particle such as אֲשֶׁר, or the like.

Sentences denoting the purpose or object may be connected with the
principal clause by a combination of the relative with *libbu* "heart," "middle,"
or even by means of *ina libbi* without the relative construction, which Dr.
Schrader has aptly compared with the use of the Hebrew לְמַעַן. We find, for
instance, *ina libbi tumaŝi-sunutav* "in order that thou learn them" (N. R. 27),
libbû sa Gumātav agasū Magu-su bita attu-nu la issu'u "in order that that Gomates
the Magian might not destroy our house." *Anama sa* is employed in the
same sense, as at Behistun (21) *anama sa la yumaŝŝunu* "in order that they
might not learn." These, however, were all expedients that belonged to the
Achæmenian age of Assyria; in the older inscriptions such clauses as those we
are now considering were expressed by the preposition *ana* and an infinitive,
in full analogy with Hebrew, Aramaic, and Ethiopic. This construction
is also found on the Persian monuments; *ana ebis limsu*, for instance, being
"in order to make a tablet." *Sa* and *assu* are also found sometimes in the
place of *ana;* thus *sa limnu la bane panim* means "in order that the evil-doer
may not make head," *assum aibi la bane panim* "in order that the wicked may
not make head."

Two kinds of subordinate sentences are now alone left for our notice.
A sentence may be temporal, denoting the time at which the event recorded
in the principal sentence took place. We have already seen that where
one event followed as a consequence upon another the Assyrians adopted a
construction that reminds us very forcibly of the Hebrew *waw consecutivum*.
We have seen also that *sa* might be occasionally used in a temporal sense.
But the chief particle that served for this purpose was *ci;* as at Naksh-i-
Rustam (20), *ci imuru* "when he had seen." It was through its temporal
sense that *ci* came to have a conditional one, as in the statement *ci tagabbū*
"if thou sayest" (N. R. 25). The sense of "until" was expressed by *adi* with
the future, as in *adi allacu* "until I shall go" (Sm. *A.*, 125, 67); and in
the Achæmenian period by the compound *adi 'eli sa*, which, however, had a
more conditional meaning than the simple *adi*. Thus at Behistun (47) we
have *adi 'eli sa anacu allacu ana mat Madai* "until I should go (or, "have gone")

to the country of the Medes." With the construct aorist the compound con-junction had the sense of "whilst;" e.g., *adi 'eli sa agā ebus* "whilst I did this" (N. R. 32). We may compare the Hebrew עַד אֲשֶׁר or עַד לְ. The other kind of sentence to which I refer is one which may be termed corre-lative, an example of which is quoted by Prof. Schrader from Behistun (104), in the shape of *ul anacu ul zirya* "neither I nor my seed." An affirmative sentence of the kind is formed, as in Hebrew, by the repetition of the conjunc-tion *va*.

Perhaps we should not pass over a very common form of sentence in Assyrian, in which a quotation is introduced by *umma* "thus," answering to the Greek ὅτι, the Aramaic דִ, the Arabic *'an*, and the Ethiopic *cama* or *ysma*. Instances will be: *igabbi umma anacu sar Elami* " he says that ' I (am) king of Elam'" (Beh. 30), *(Istar) ciham ikbi-sunut umma anacu allac ina makhar Assur-bani-pal* " (Istar) thus said to them that ' I am going in the presence of Assur-bani-pal'" (Sm. *A.*, 221, 2, 4), *ciham ikbuni umma temenna suati nubahi la nimur* "thus they had said that ' this foundation-stone we sought, we could not see'" (*W. A. I.* I., 69, 2, 55). The frequent combination of the two particles, *ciham* at the beginning of the sentence and *umma* at its end, should be observed. *Ciham* is very common in the inscriptions of the Achæmenian period, whereas its employment in the older texts is rare.

Before concluding this lecture I would call your attention to the use of the Assyrian passive participle, to express the sense of "able to be" or "ought to be," as *ana siri sarri* "a gate ought to be begun" (*W. A. I.* III., 53, 2). The Pael participles of concave verbs more especially bear this meaning: thus *dicu* is "what can be slain," *la niba* "what cannot be counted," *pu'u 'ussuru* "a mouth that should be bound." Perhaps, too, a few words might be said about the use of some of the prepositions; the ideas of "change," "result," or "object," for instance, are denoted by *ana* with the accusative, as in *ana tulle u simmi itur* "to mounds and ruins it turned," *ana suzub napsati-sun ipparsidu* "to save their lives they fled." *Ina*, again, has the signification of "into" after a verb which means "to descend," and *ultu* is occasionally used adverbially for "after that," "from the time when," with *yumi sa* "the day whereon" understood. Thus in the "Descent of Istar" (*Rev.* 16) we read *ultu libba-sa inikhu* "after that her heart had rested,"[1] *istu*

---

[1] Or rather, "she had rested in her heart," the verb being in the masculine instead of the feminine.

ibná-ni Maruduc "from the time when Merodach created me." *Ultu* may also signify "exacting punishment from," as in *ultu Assuri tirra ducte abi* "from Assyria bring back the slaughter of (thy) father," that is to say, "avenge upon Assyria thy father's death."

What has been said will make it plain how closely the syntax of the Assyrian language agrees with that of the other Semitic tongues. In some respects, indeed, it is even simpler and more primitive, and in its temporal use of *ci* approaches the idiom of our modern languages. Thought, as expressed in the sentence, must be either predicative or objective, and the simplest form of the sentence must be much the same in all languages. The connection of ideas when reduced to its most necessary elements admits of but little variation. It is only when the sentence becomes developed and complicated, and more especially when two sentences are brought into relation one with another, that syntactical differences on any large scale become possible. But the syntax even of the simplest sentence is not necessarily the same in all families of speech. Subject and predicate, or subject verb and object, admit of varying arrangement, and while some languages (like the Polynesian) do not possess a verb at all, others (like the Semitic dialects) possess only what is on its way towards becoming a verb. Even mere predication may be conceived of differently by different races of men, and accordingly the original Aryan conception which placed the predicate before the word it defined (as "good man," "man's good") is reversed in the Semitic languages, where adjective and genitive must follow the subject. Since the predicative sentence easily passes into the objective sentence, "man is mortal," for instance, being the same as "man possesses mortality," we find that the relative position of the subject and object is determined by that of the subject and predicate. In the Aryan languages the governed word was primarily placed before the word that governed it, just as the predicate was before its subject. Similarly in the Semitic languages we should expect to find the objective sentence following the rule of the predicative sentence, and making the object succeed the verb. I need only point to Hebrew to prove how familiar this order was to the Semitic mind, and numberless examples of it occur in Assyrian. In the latter language, however, it must be confessed that the reverse arrangement had become predominant, the verb being relegated to the end of the sentence. In this we may, perhaps, see the effects of Accadian influence, the Accadian verb regularly standing after its case. Should this suggestion be correct, we shall have the evidence of comparative syntax also for the fact which is borne out by the accidence and the lexicon,—the influence, namely, exerted by the old agglutinative language of Chaldea upon the Semitic dialects which superseded it.

LECTURE IX.

The Affinities of the Assyrian Language and the Origin of Semitic Culture.

NOW that we have finished our review of the Assyrian syllabary and grammar, we can look about us, and consider the conclusions to which we have been led. Assyrian, we have seen, is a Semitic language which made use of a foreign mode of writing, and, like the Japanese, which has similarly borrowed the Chinese characters, had to adapt it to the expression of its sounds as best it could. The Accadian inventors of the syllabary spoke an agglutinative tongue, and since the characters they employed were originally nothing more than hieroglyphics or ideographs, they will inform us what objects and ideas were known at the time they were invented, and consequently what degree of civilisation had already been reached. The Semitic population which succeeded the people of Accad was inferior in culture, and accordingly borrowed largely from the old race. Not only the system of writing, but the Accadian literature, along with the elements of Accadian art and science, became the property of the new comers. So extensive a borrowing necessarily left its marks on the language of the borrowers, and we shall therefore expect to find in Assyrian numerous words which were taken from the alien speech. But when two languages exist side by side for any length of time, the influence of that spoken by the more civilised race is likely to extend beyond the mere vocabulary; phonology, idiom and even grammar are all apt to be affected. I have already had occasion to point out that this seems to have been the case with Assyrian; the interchange of *m* and *v*, so characteristic of Accadian, is to be found in Assyrian also, and the appearance of something like real tenses in the Assyrian verb is best explained by Accadian influence. Of course, the borrowing was not all on one side; during the long period when the two races dwelt close together the Accadians borrowed many words, such as *bansur* (Ass. *passuru*) "a dish," *kharub* "a locust," *succal*(?) "a messenger," *isib* "a settlement," *adama* "the red race," from their neighbours, and Semitic influence will best account for the fact that the Accadian verb which originally postfixed the pronouns came afterwards to prefix them, while the adjective followed its substantive instead of preceding it as was once the case.[1]

The Semitic inhabitants of Babylonia are called Casdim in the Old Testament, a word which I would connect with the common Assyrian *casadu* "to possess" or "conquer." The Casdim would, accordingly, be the Assyrian *cásidi* or "conquerors," who first made their appearance in Sumir or Shinar, that is to say, north-western Chaldea, at some unknown period before the second millenium B.C.[2] The language of these Casdim was what is termed Assyrian, though the Assyrians were merely a part of the nation which migrated northward about 1800 B.C., and the Assyrian language merely a dialect of the Babylonian from which it differed but slightly. A comparison of the Assyrian and Accadian lexicons, by disclosing the debt of the former to the latter, ought to indicate in some measure the amount of civilisation possessed by the Semitic Babylonians when they first came into contact with the Accadian race.

Here we are confronted by the question: what is the relation of the Semitic dialect of Babylonia, whether we call it Babylonian, or Assyrian, or anything else, to the other dialects of the Semitic family of speech? Is it most closely allied to the northern Semitic tongues, Hebrew, Phœnician and Aramaic, or to the southern, Arabic, Himyaritic, and Ethiopic? The question can only be answered by an appeal to the grammar and dictionary, but more especially to the grammar.

From time to time I have had to draw your attention to the analogies

---

[1] Many of the words given in the syllabaries as borrowed from the Semites do not appear in the Accadian texts, and must have been confined to the literary class of a later day, which was partly Accadian, partly Semitic. Thus *ibila* from the Assyrian *'ablu*, was employed in the place of the native *dumu* (*dū*) or *tur*, "a son;" perhaps, too, *libis* "a heart," from the Assyrian *libbi-su* "his heart," instead of the native *sini* or *sā*.

[2] The position of Sumir or Shinar is fixed by Gen. x. 10, which places in it Babylon and Erech, the great cities of north-western Chaldea. Accad, on the other hand, is sometimes called Uru or Uri (*W. A. I.* III., 70, 154), from its capital Ur (now Mugheir) in the south on the western bank of the Euphrates.

existing between the grammar of Assyrian and those of the other Semitic idioms, but particularly that of Hebrew. And, in fact, it is to Hebrew that Assyrian is most akin. In the first place the phonology of the two languages agrees in a remarkable manner. The sibilants are not changed into dentals as in Aramaic and Arabic, and though we sometimes find שׁ and ס changing places in Hebrew and Assyrian, this is not the case with the majority of roots. In Assyrian itself, moreover, certain words are found now with ס, now with שׁ, while we all remember that the northern Israelites were distinguished from their southern brethren by their preference for the sound of *samech* (Jud. xii. 6). Then in the second place, there is a striking agreement between the grammatical forms of Hebrew and Assyrian. The Niphal conjugation characterises both, and though the use of the secondary conjugations with inserted *t* has attained larger proportions in Assyrian, the Hebrew Hithpael proves that the starting-point of the two languages must have been the same, Assyrian merely developing what Hebrew restricted in use. Indeed, in our comparison of forms we must never forget that the Hebrew of the Old Testament is a very attenuated speech. It has lost forms which it must once have possessed and has undergone to a large extent the action of phonetic decay. Traces of the case-endings are still to be found in it. The accusative of direction in הָ־ still retains the long vowel which has been shortened in Assyrian, and the nominative in וֹ— and genitive in יֹ— are still to be met with in scattered passages, such as Gen. i. 24; Num. xxiv. 3, 15; Psa. cxiv. 8; Isa. i. 21; as well as in proper names like *Bethu-el* and *Penu-el*. It is probable that the loss of the case-endings is often to be ascribed to the alphabet in which the Old Testament is written, final vowels not being expressed if they were short. At all events the inscription of Shishak, in which the local names of Palestine, like *Negebu* " Negeb," are made to terminate in a vowel, contains a clear proof that the case-endings were preserved in Hebrew not very long before the Moabite inscription of King Mesha was inscribed. In compounds like *Penuel* their presence was naturally marked in the writing, and the Hebrew accentuation which now falls for the most part on the last syllable, though analogy would require it to fall on the penultima, is further evidence of their former existence in the language. Even the mimmation may perhaps be detected in such adjectives as יוֹמָם or אָמְנָם, if we assume that they are old accusatives, and the feminine ending in *t* which has been weakened into ה in so many instances constantly reappears, as in the construct state where it has maintained itself, like the nominative-ending in *Penuel*, on account of the pronunciation which made the construct and the following genitive form together a single compound. Even Assyrian offers a few examples in which the final dental of the feminine has been dropped, or rather softened into a simple aspirate, from which we may draw the inference that the dental itself was an aspirated one. As regards the dual and plural, Assyrian has been less conservative than Hebrew; *m* has been changed to *n*, the common masculine plural has altogether lost the last consonant like the construct plural in Hebrew, and the termination of the dual has been similarly reduced to a vowel and restricted in use. In the third person plural of the verb, too, the construct aorist has dropped its final consonant (*-un*, *-an*), just as Hebrew has done, though the subjective aorist retains the older ending (*-ūni*, *-āni*), which also makes its appearance sporadically in Hebrew. Even the Shaphel is shown to have been once common in Hebrew by the crystallised forms שכן from כון, שקל from קל, etc.; elsewhere the initial sibilant has become an aspirate, as in the pronoun of the third person. The Aphel conjugation proves that the same process had begun to be at work in Assyrian also. In other respects, however, the Assyrian verb presents resemblances to the Arabic. The various forms of the aorist, the existence of a precative, of passives in *u* (like the Hebrew Pual), and of conjugations analogous to the 8th, 14th and 15th of Arabic, all remind us of the latter language. But these resemblances resolve themselves partly into the preservation of primitive forms like those of the subjective and objective aorists, partly into a similar but independent development as in the case of the artificial regularity of the conjugations.

To a later development must be assigned the Hebrew article and inseparable prepositions. No traces of an article make their appearance in Assyrian before the Achæmenian period, and the Hebrew article was probably at the outset nothing more than the demonstrative pronoun, which answered to the Assyrian *'ullu*. In the Assyrian inscriptions we already meet with the abbreviated *li* instead of *liviti* (from לוה), and *it* instead of *itti*, but except in the case of *lapani* (Heb. לפני), an inseparable preposition cannot be said to exist. The analogy of the construct feminine singular and plural and masculine plural, however, in which Hebrew and Assyrian agree exactly with

one another, might have led us to assume a parallel agreement in the case of
the masculine construct singular; but instances like *Penu-el*, which would be
pan-il(i) in Assyrian, show that this assumption would have been incorrect.
The Hebrew usage in which the vowel-endings are preserved must have been
the original one, since in Arabic it is only the nunnation and the final -*ni* of
the dual and -*na* of the *pluralis sanus* which are lost before the genitive. It is
probable, therefore, that the shortened pronunciation which caused the loss of
the terminations of the first noun acted primarily on the dual and plural, and
was afterwards extended by analogy to the singular. So far as the feminine
singular was concerned, the loss must have occurred before the Assyrians and
Hebrews parted company with one another; the masculine construct singular,
however, would have preserved its case-endings, though not its mimmation,
until a subsequent period.

If now we turn to the lexicon, we shall find the most striking agreement
between Assyrian on the one side and Hebrew on the other. Such an agreement will be looked for in vain between Assyrian and any other Semitic
language, with the exception, of course, of Phœnician, which is practically
identical with Hebrew. But even where Phœnician and Hebrew differ in their
use of words, we find Assyrian agreeing rather with the latter than with the
former; thus "foot" is *raglu*, רגל, and not פעם; "good" is *dhabu*, טוב, not
נעם, and the root כון "to establish," has not passed into the general idea of
"existence," as in Phœnician, Æthiopic, and Arabic. Not unfrequently, however, words that are archaic or poetical in Hebrew are common both in
Phœnician and Assyrian; this is the case with *alpu*, (אלף) "an ox," instead
of שור; *arkhu*, "a month," (ירח) instead of חדש; or *pilu*, "worked," (פעל)
instead of עשה. So, too, Phœnician coincides with Assyrian in its use of the
participle as a tense, as well as of the relative ש (*sa*) instead of אשר. This
relative, however, was also employed in the northern dialect of Hebrew, as
may be seen from the books of Judges and Canticles.

Aramaic, the remaining member of the North Semitic group, stands at
a great distance from Assyrian. Indeed, it differs from Assyrian in almost
all those points in which it differs from Hebrew. Its phonology has undergone
a considerable change, a good many of the sibilants having become dentals,
while *tsaddi* has sometimes passed into ע. In the Aramaic ערע and תרין it
is difficult to recognise the Assyrian *irtsi(tuv)*, and *sanu'u*, or the Hebrew ארץ

and שנים. Though the consonantal system of Assyrian itself has undergone considerable modification, as we have seen in an earlier lecture, *kheth* being frequently omitted and *s* changing into *l* before a dental, in all the points in which Aramaic has departed from the primitive Semitic phonology, Assyrian remains true to the earlier sounds. On the other hand it must be allowed that the latter language resolves a final ה into *u*, just as Aramaic does into א, while the guttural sound of ע, so characteristic of Hebrew, is almost, if not entirely, unknown to Assyrian. But the "emphatic aleph" or postfixed article of the Aramaic idioms, has nothing analogous in the language of Nineveh, and implies a previous loss of the case-endings. The preservation of a Shaphel conjugation is one of the marks of archaism which Aramaic shares with Assyrian; the formation of the precative, being common to Arabic and Ethiopic, as well as to Aramaic and Assyrian, would also go back to the period that preceded the separation of the Semitic tribes; and the periphrastic genitive is found in all the Semitic tongues. The loss of the emphatic aleph in the construct state is easily explicable from its origin, and is not to be compared with the loss of the Assyrian case-endings in the same position, while the Assyrian use of *ana* with the accusative, and the mode in which the superlative is denoted, belong to the later period of the language when it had been affected by Aramaic influences. The employment of *di*, the passives in *eth*, the want of a Niphal, the dropping of the vowels, the extension given to the formation of abstracts, the use of compound tenses, and of the substantive verb אות instead of יש (*isu*), all draw a clear line of demarcation between the idiom of Syria and that of Assyria. The vocabulary, too, points in the same direction. "Man," in Assyrian, is *admu*, (אדם) rather than אנש; "to take," is לקח, rather than קבל; "king," is מלך, rather than שלט; while the specifically Aramaic בר, "son," is replaced by *'ablu*, (יבל) and *binu* (בן).[1] Aramaic must have separated from its sister-dialects and entered upon an independent course of development long before the ancestors of the Hebrews and the Phœnicians had quitted their kinsfolk in Babylonia. And this is borne out by tradition. The Phœnicians believed that they had originally migrated from

[1] At the same time, as might have been expected from their proximity, the vocabularies of Aram and Assyria contain a considerable number of words in common. Thus we have the Assyrian *elippu* (*elipu*), "a ship," Aram. אלפא; *matu*, "country" (of Accadian derivation), Aram. מתא; *igáru*, "heap," Aram. יגרא; and Dr. Delitzsch notices that the Assyrian *talimu* is the Samaritan *tellem*, "full brother," and the Aram. *telâma*, which we have also in the proper name Bartholomew ("son of Talmai"). See, also, Num. xiii. 22.

the Persian Gulf,[1] Kepheus ruled in Chaldea, according to one legend, and at
Joppa according to another, and the Israelites never forgot that their father
Abram had been born at " Ur of the Chaldees."   But we look in vain for any
traces of a similar tradition amongst the mountainous tribes of Aram, or
Subarti, the "highlands" as it was called in Accadian.   There was, it is true,
an early connection between Babylonia and Kharran, which is itself an
Accadian name, meaning, "the road ;" *Dun-cun-uddu*, or Mercury, is termed
"the spirit of the men of Kharran " (*W. A. I.* III., 67, 28) ; and Sargon
declares that he had restored "the decrees of Assyria and Kharran, which from
distant days had been set aside, and their laws neglected " (Botta, 144, 11) ;
but we need not look beyond the statement in Gen. xxxi. 47, to see that an
essential difference was felt to exist between Aram and Canaan.   It has
long been recognised that the table in Gen. x. is geographical rather than
ethnological, arranging the nations of western Asia according to their
position, not according to their descent.

At the same time, Aramaic belongs rather to the northern branch of the
Semitic family than to the southern, which comprises the Arabian of central
Arabia, and the Himyaritic or Sabean of Yemen, along with the Gheez or
Ethiopic of Abyssinia.   The characteristic feature of the southern group is
the existence of broken plurals, originally collective singulars, which are
altogether wanting in the northern section of the family.   The vocabulary,
again, marks the southern branch off from the northern, and we may point to
the name of the numeral " six," which retains its medial dental in Arabic and
Ethiopic (*shadash*), as a further evidence of the same fact.   The consonantal
system of the southern group, moreover, differs from that of the northern in
having developed new sounds.   Arabic, however, has been singularly conservative in regard to its nominal and verbal forms : the mimmation has
become a nunnation, though preserved in one of the dialects of the Himyaritic
inscriptions, and the three case-endings may still be heard, it is said, from the
lips of the Bedouin.   The modified forms of the imperfect or aorist, the
passives in -*u*, the use of the participle, the adverbs in -*ā*, the dual in the verb,
the secondary conjugations in *t* and *tan*, and the simplicity of the vowels, are
all so many archaisms which Arabic shares with Assyrian.   In Assyrian they

[1] Strabo, i. 2, 35 ; xvi. 3, 4 ; 4, 27 ; Justin, xviii. 3, 2 ; Pliny, *H. N.*, iv. 36 ; Herodotus, i. 1 ; vii. 89 ;
Schol. to Hom., *Od.*, iv. 84.

were stereotyped by becoming part of a literary language; in Arabic they have been preserved by the nature of the country and the unmixed blood of the speakers. But even Arabic has not been free from the action of phonetic decay and other causes of change. To say nothing of the broken plurals or the contracted forms of the third person plural of the verb, an article has grown up as in Hebrew; auxiliary tenses have come into use; the accent has been uniformly thrown back as in the Latin language, or the Æolic dialect of Greece; and the cases have fallen away in the dual and plural, -āni and -aini being alone left in the dual, and -ūna and -īna in the plural.

If we now turn to Ethiopic we shall find several points in which it agrees remarkably with Assyrian, while at the same time preserving its character as a member of the southern group of Semitic tongues. In the first place, the imperfect has been differentiated into two tenses, one yĕngĕr, the Assyrian iscun, and the other yĕnágĕr, the Assyrian isácin. In the second place, the first person singular of the perfect is formed, as in Assyrian, by the guttural (gabarcu), though in the second person where Ethiopic has again a guttural, Assyrian has the dental of the other northern dialects. Then thirdly, the tens in both Ethiopic and Assyrian are characterised by the same suffix ā (e.g., ĕsrā, Ass. isrā " 20," salasā, Ass. silasâ " 30 "), and Dr. Schrader notices that it is in Ethiopic and Assyrian alone, that the old plural ending in -an is shortened to -ā when a noun is used with a numeral denoting one of the tens. Add to this the existence of an Istaphal, of adverbs in -a, of a suffix -tu or -ti, and of verbal nouns like mafrey (corresponding with the Assyrian manzazu), and we have a series of remarkable resemblances between the two languages. The violent letter-change and peculiar prepositions, too, which distinguish Ethiopic, are analogous to what we meet with in Assyrian. These resemblances, how- ever, may all be explained as resulting either from the preservation of old forms which must once have been possessed by all the Semitic idioms, or from the action of similar circumstances, Ethiopic, like Assyrian, being an offlying branch of the Semitic stock brought into close contact with an unallied language. The two forms iscun and isácin must have been a common heritage of the Semitic family, while the first personal pronoun an-acu shows that the form gabarcu or sacnacu is at least as old as the form kabaltu or kâbalti. The Ethiopic, or Sabean section, would have been separated from the parent speech while the perfect or permansive was still in the process of making, and

for reasons which it is impossible to discover, Assyrian alone of all the dialects
which were left behind continued to prefer the formation with the guttural to
that with the dental. As for the mimmation and the retention of the initial
sibilant in the third personal pronoun, which characterise one of the Himyaritic dialects, they are simply survivals from the primitive past.

This brief sketch of the relations of Assyrian to the cognate languages
will have abundantly illustrated its importance for the study of comparative
Semitic grammar, and the light thrown by it upon the parent Semitic speech.
Thus all doubt has been removed in regard to the original existence of the
case-endings in all the Semitic dialects, and I have already endeavoured to
trace the genesis of the tenses of the verb by the help of Assyrian, while I
hope hereafter to show by the same means, that the accentuation of Ethiopic
approaches more nearly that of the parent-speech than does the accentuation
of any other Semitic tongue, Assyrian alone excepted. We are taken back to
a time when as yet there was no verb, or rather no distinction between noun
and verb, when the relative and the periphrastic genitive did not exist, when
the noun was provided with a mimmation as well as a vocalic case-ending
which was not yet dropped in the construct state, when the plural terminated
in -*āmu*, used alike of masculine and feminine nouns, and when the accent
fell, for the most part, on the final or penultimate syllables of the word. When
once the reconstruction of primitive Semitic grammar has been made fairly
complete, we may proceed to compare it with Old Egyptian or the sub-Semitic
dialects of northern Africa, and determine how far the resemblances that
seem to exist between Semitic and African grammar are illusory or founded
on fact.

But important as Assyrian is for comparative grammar, it is equally
important for a reconstruction of the primitive Semitic dictionary, and thereby
of primitive Semitic culture. If once we know by the help of comparison
what words were possessed by the Semites before their separation, we shall
have a clue to the degree of civilisation they had reached. We cannot, it is
true, infer from the absence of any words in the later dialects that they had
never been possessed by the parent-speech ; what we can infer is, that where
such words can be proved to exist, the objects or ideas they represent must
have been known. And the Assyrian inscriptions take us back to a time
when Semitic civilisation was growing up under the fostering influences of

Accad. The records of the teachers of the Semitic race have come down to us, written in their own language and embodying their own thoughts. And when we have proof that a Semitic word has been borrowed from the Accadian, we are justified in believing that the object or idea which it signified was borrowed also. Dr. Schrader has long ago noticed that the parallelism which characterises the poetry of the northern Semites has its prototype in the poetry of Accad, and the epical literature of Babylonia and Assyria certainly had its source in that of the Accadians. The debts incurred by the Semitic lexicon and culture may be illustrated by a few examples. We should expect, however, to find the debt largest in the case of the Assyrians, and next to them in that of the northern Semites, the southern Semites of Arabia being least affected by the Turanian civilisation of the Euphrates valley; and such turns out to be the fact.

The city is the first requisite of settled and civilised life. The walled πόλις with its temples, its marketplace, and its baths, was to the Greeks the sign and symbol of an organised state. But the Semite, uninfluenced by favouring circumstances, has ever been a nomade and a wanderer. The Bedouin of Arabia is the purest specimen of Semitic blood with whom we can meet, Hebrew tradition brings the patriarchs before us as roving shepherds, and the " wandering Jew " is still a representative of the best part of the Semitic race. A pastoral life and trade, these have been the two passions of the Semites from the earliest times. It is instructive to compare the history of the mixed population of Babylonia, which preferred to live quietly at home occupied with agriculture and learning, with that of the purer Assyrian, whose armies overran the larger portion of western Asia with little other object than the mere desire of traversing the earth. Now the word for " city " (עיר) which is found in Hebrew and Aramaic, and probably forms part of the name of Jeru-salem, is not met with in Assyrian except as a proper name. This is *Uru*, now represented by the mounds of Mugheir, the Ur of Genesis where Abraham was born. But Uru was of Accadian origin. It was, in fact, the capital of Accad, or south-eastern Babylonia, and it obeyed the rule of Accadian princes long after Sumir or Shinar had fallen into Semitic hands. *Uru* meant simply " the city," and under another form, that of *eri*, or rather *öri*,[1]

---

[1] The original form of *eri* is given as *erim*, and translated by the Assyrian *isittu*, "foundation." *Erim* was adopted by the Assyrians under the form of *erimmātu*, and with the special sense of "boundary-stone."

must have been borrowed by the ancestors of the Hebrews and Aramæans before their migration to the west. Like many other Accadian words which originally began with the syllable *mu*, *Uru* has lost its initial consonant, *muru* becoming first *wuru* and then *'uru*. The definite case *murub*, however, formed by the demonstrative pronoun *bi*, has preserved the original labial.[1]

While the Aramæans and Hebrews took with them not only the Accadian conception of city life, but also the name the Accadians gave to it, the Assyrians, or rather the Semitic Babylonians of Shinar, had adapted a word of their own to the same purpose. This word was *ālu*, the Hebrew אהל "a tent," the tent of the nomade being changed into the city of the settled burgher. The southern Semite remained ignorant of both conception and word, and when he afterwards began to build his towns and to call them by a special name, it was one which had no connection with the civilisation of ancient Accad.

But the existence of the city brought with it new conceptions and consequently new names. The shepherd or the trader had all the world before him; he recognised neither boundaries nor landed possessions; the desert was limitless and the Semite was free to wander where he would. Settled life, however, brought with it the recognition of property, the limitation of landed rights, and the demarcation of state and nation. The Assyrian term for "country," *matu*, as opposed to *irtsitu* (ארץ) "the earth," was one borrowed immediately from Accad. The Accadian *ma*, " land," was extended into *mada* by the individualising affix *da;* and while *ma* represented " country " in general, *mada* was some one country in particular. Through the general decay that affected the terminations of Accadian words *mada* came to be contracted into *mad*, and this when adopted by the Semites was furnished with a feminine termination, and so became successively *madătu*, *madtu*, *mattu*, and *mātu*. The Aramæans carried the word away with them under the form of מתא, from which we must infer that the borrowing had taken place before the separation of the northern Semitic tribes. Pre-Aryan Media, the cradle of the Accadian race, probably received its name from this word *mada*, and the " Median " dynasty of Berosus, which has formed the basis of so many historical and

---

[1] *W. A. I.* II., 30, 17. It is possible, however, that *murub* here denotes "the woman" (Assyrian *'uru*, הרה), regarded as "the conceiver."

ethnological theories, may really have owed its title to the "land" of Shinar or Accad from which it came.

Nanga "a district," is another word which made its way from Accadian to Assyrian, where it took the form of *nagû*. Since Accadian *ng* between two vowels presupposes an earlier *m*, we may restore the original form of the word as *nama*. The word belonged also to the dialect of southern Elam if we are to judge from the names of the cities Nagitu and Nagiti-dihiban, at the mouth of the Eulæus, to which Merodach-Baladan fled for refuge.

The terms applied by the Semitic Babylonians to the foundations of their brick buildings were naturally borrowed from their Accadian instructors. Thus *epinu* "foundation," is the Accadian *äpin* (contracted into *pin*), and *temennu* "a foundation-stone," is the Accadian *timmena* (i.e., *timena*) which was successively weakened into *timmen*, *timme*, *tim* or *tem*, and *te*. It is curious that, while the Accadians called their Semitic invaders by a name of native origin, *lugud* "the white race," from *luga* or *lugur* "man" (possibly for *muluga*), and *ud* or *uda* "white," they adopted from their enemies the name of *adamatu* "the red race," by which they were themselves called, under the form of *adama*. The Accadian language showed the same dislike to the pronunciation of a final consonant as does modern French, and *adama* stands for *adamat*. We can hardly refuse to accept the old opinion which connected אדם "man," the Assyrian *admu*, with the root which means to be "red :" in this case the Adam of scripture would appear to have been Accadian just as much as "the sons of Elohim" (Gen. vi. 2,) to have belonged to the "white" Semitic race.

Ippu or *ibbu*, the Hebrew יפה, was, however, the usual Assyrian word for "white," and it answered to the Accadian *uknu* "crystal-white." Just as the feminines *adamătu* or *tenisetu* (אנוש), are used to express the abstract conceptions of "red race" and "mankind," so the feminine *ippatu* would be employed in the sense of "the white race." Now *ippatu* corresponds letter for letter with the Biblical יפת or Japhet, and the question accordingly arises whether the name of Japhet does not denote that he was the forefather of the "white" Aryan race. M. Harkavy suggested some time ago that the name Japhet was to be connected with that of Mount *Niphates*, and the Aryan root *snigh*, from which we find νίφα "snow" in Greek, and *nix* in Latin. The suggestion is confirmed by the fact that חם Ham, the father of the swarthy

11

Africans, seems to get his name from the root חום (חמם), حَمّ "to be black (hot)," the Coptic *kham* or *kam*, while *Shem* must, I think, be connected with the Assyrian *samu* "brownish." '*Samu* also appears under the form of *sihamu*, with which the Hebrew שהם must be allied, Assyrian *s* answering here to Hebrew ש as in many other instances. Even in Assyrian itself we have *sibitti*, "seven," by the side of *sibitti*; *sarru*, by the side of *sarru*. '*Samu* is applied to any neutral colour: a blue mist or cloud is called *samu*, just as much as a dark-green stone or a yellow flower. '*Samu* is also given as the equivalent of *adru*, "dark," from which comes the name of the cloudy winter month Adar, as well as *adirtu*, "an eclipse."

Now both *samu* and *adru* are, I believe, of Accadian derivation. A syllabary (*W. A. I.* II., 1. 177, 178) tells us that ⟨cuneiform⟩ when sounded *dir* in Accadian represented the Assyrian *adru*, and when sounded *sa* the Assyrian *sa'amu*; and elsewhere the same character is rendered by *khalapu* and *sutruru*, "covered," and *mikit-isati*, "the burning of fire." Just as the original form of the Accadian *pin* was *äpin*, so the original form of *dir* may have been *adir*, from which the Semitic *adiru*, *adru* would have been derived; at all events the general analogy of Accadian phonology leads us to infer an earlier form, *sam* for *sa*, from which *sa'amu* (and then the weakened *sihamu*) was borrowed.[1] It is a familiar common-place that semi-barbarous peoples are unable to distinguish between any but the most obvious colours; to this day the same word means both "blue" and "green" in Welsh, and the Homeric πορφύρεος, οἶνοψ, and the like, are of the vaguest possible signification. A nice appreciation of tints shows a fairly advanced state of civilisation. If, then, the Semites received their first lessons in the art of distinguishing accurately between colours from the more cultured Accadian, it would only be what we should expect. And the Semitic name of another colour, yellow, seems equally referable to an Accadian source. In *W. A. I.* II., 26, 56-55, *ara* is given together with *sizi* as the Accadian equivalent of the Assyrian *arku* "green" or "yellow," and *urik* as the equivalent of *urcitu* "verdure," while *khir* is further translated by the Assyrian *arku*. A comparison of the three forms enables us to restore the original *khirik*, which became *khir*, *urik* and

[1] In *W. A. I.* II., 26, 47, *samanu* has been placed in the Accadian column either by mistake, or else because it had been borrowed by the Accadians from the Semites after the establishment of the latter in Shinar. In the preceding line *gug* is given as the Accadian for "blue;" compare the Tatar *kuk*, "blue;" and Protomedic *an-cic*, "divine blue," or "sky."

ara, the Semites adopting the word while it was still pronounced *khirik* or *urik*. The adoption must certainly go back to a very early time, as the word in some form or other is to be found in the southern as well as in the northern Semitic dialects. In Ethiopic, indeed, it has given a name to "gold" (*warĕk*).

Another word which was borrowed by the Semites while they still encamped on the western banks of the Euphrates, before their separation, was the Accadian *ega* "a crown." Royalty and its insignia were of Accadian, not of Semitic growth; the Semite was by nature a democrat. *Mir* was used in the same sense in Accadian, and was also applied to the "halo" seen surrounding the moon in cloudy weather; *ega*, however, was the only term adopted by the Semitic nomads. From it we have not only the Assyrian *agû*, "a crown," but various words signifying round objects, out of which was finally developed the Arabic verb عال "to be round."

The "great king" himself ruled over Accad before he ruled over Semitic Shinar. The Hebrew שׂר is the Assyrian *sarru*, with this difference, that whereas in Hebrew מלך is "rex," and שׂר merely "regulus," the converse is the case in Assyrian. Now the Assyrian *sarru* must, I believe, be referred to an Accadian origin. 'Sa in that language means "to judge," and ⟨⊨⟩ ∀ which we are informed by glosses is to be pronounced either *sa-galum* or *sa-gar*, literally, "judgment-maker," signifies "monarch." But from *sa* might also be formed *sara* by the suffix *-ra*, and we find ⧉⊟ accordingly pronounced in Accadian as *sara*, and rendered by the Assyrian *sarrû*. It does not need to be pointed out that the derivation of *sarru* (שׂרר), originally a monosyllable and so contrary to the general character of Semitic roots, is most obviously to be sought in *sara*. We shall thus be able to understand how it came about that the Babylonians and Assyrians who inherited immediately the traditions of Accadian culture, used *sarru* in its Accadian sense, while the more distant Hebrews allowed the native מלך to take its place. It must be remembered, however, that a favourite title of both Accadian and Semitic princes was *ri'u*, Accadian *siba*, "a shepherd" (רעה), which reminds us of the Homeric ποιμὴν λαῶν, while according to Berosus, Alorus, the first of the antediluvian kings, assumed the title of "shepherd." Such a title certainly suits a pastoral race of nomads better than the organised communities of pre-Semitic Chaldea.

However this may be, the conceptions connected with the regular administration of law might be expected to have emanated from Accad, where it was carried to high perfection, and where, as we have seen, his judicial office gave the monarch one of his titles. We need not be surprised, therefore, at finding the semi-monosyllabic דן (דון) "judge," claiming a non-Semitic parentage. The Accadian *di* is the equivalent of the Assyrian *dinu* "a judge" (*W. A. I.* II., 7, 32), and *di* in Accadian presupposes an earlier *din* and a still earlier *dim(ä)*, like *du* (*dun, dum*) "to go," and other words. The earliest code of laws of which we know is an Accadian one, and the legal phraseology and procedure of Accad was very complete.

A good idea of the organised administration of the country may be obtained from a bilingual tablet given in *W. A. I.* II., 38, 1 *Rev.* Here we find that "the payer of tribute" (*da-lu-u sa bil-ti*) had a distinct name, though unfortunately only the two last characters, *ci-ta*, of the Accadian word are left. So, too, had "the defaulter" or *khi-bu-u*, whose name is written ideographically in Accadian "the man who makes default," and without any clue to its pronunciation; and the "tax-payer" or *ra-pi-ku*, with which the Aramaic רבק may be connected, was similarly described in the Accadian mode of writing, as "the man who makes payment" (LUGUR AL GARA). After the defaulter comes "the taxgatherer," *ma-ci-su* in Assyrian, like the Arabic مكس, whose Accadian title was, "the man who makes execution" (*lugur gar-tar-da garà*). Next follows "the commissioner of the brickyards," *la-bi-in la-bit-ti*, a very important personage in a country which depended so largely for writing as well as for building purposes upon its native clay. His Accadian title we have no means of reading; it is ideographically written, LUGUR MUR ZI-GAB, "the man who oversees the bricks." After him we have "the collector of the taxes," *la-kidh kur-ba-an-ni*, where it is interesting to find the *corban* of the New Testament employed in the sense of "taxation." The Accadian equivalent is D.P. lak[1] RIRIGA which bears the same sense. The alien was termed *a-si-bu*, "the squatter," in Assyrian, and LUGUR CA-CA-MA, "the man told over," in Accadian, while the burgher was *ca-tu-u* in Assyrian, and LUGUR CA GINA, "the man of the fixed face," in Accadian. The "tribute" paid by subject populations was called in Accadian, *gun*, which is written phonetically ⬦⬦ ⊨||⊬ *gu-un*. The word may be allied to the verb *gin*, or *gen*, "to establish."

With all their culture, however, the Accadians were an agricultural rather

[1] See *W. A. I.* II., 2, 373.

than a commercial people, and though we hear of "ships of Ur" (*W. A. I.* II., 46, 3), trade does not seem to have been in a very developed state until after the Semitic conquest. Even the usual word for "price," *sam*, was borrowed by the Accadians from their Semitic neighbours. On the other hand, the old population of Chaldea was famous from an early period for its mathematical studies, its astronomical observations, its astrology and its magic, and in the case of all these we should expect to find that the Semites had borrowed largely, not only ideas, but the words which expressed them as well. Our expectation will not be disappointed. As I noticed several years ago in my *Assyrian Grammar for Comparative Purposes*, the Semitic term for "one hundred," מאה, Assyrian *me*, is of Accadian origin. While the Accadians used a convenient system of cyphers for all numbers under one hundred, they represented the latter numeral by ⫫, *me*, the ideograph of "assemblage." *Me* is a contracted form of *eme* "a tongue," of which the ideograph was originally a drawing, and hence it means, "a voice," "to call," and "an assemblage." But it is also a contracted form of *mes*, "many," which frequently marks the plural in Accadian, like *mas* in Protomedic, *me* itself performing the same function in Susianian. *Me* further signified "one hundred," but whether as a later abbreviation of *eme* or of *mes* I cannot say. Since מאה is common to all the Semitic idioms it must be one of those words which were adopted by the Semites before their separation, when they had not as yet crossed the Euphrates. This is not the case with another word, the Assyrian *estin*, "one," which Dr. Delitzsch has traced with great probability to an Accadian source.[1] This is the Accadian *as*, "one," with the usual suffix *ta-a-an* "sum," or "number." *Estin* makes its appearance in Hebrew in the name of "eleven," *'ashtê âsâr*, and we may perhaps infer that the word was borrowed only by the northern branch of Semites. An example of the debts incurred by the Semitic dictionary to the Accadian in the matter of magic will be found in the Hebrew אוב, primarily a "familiar spirit," and then, "one who has a familiar spirit."[2] The Assyrian equivalent is *ubutu*, or *abutu*, "magic," which, as M. Lenormant first noticed, comes from the Accadian *ubi* "the calling up of a ghost."

It is needless to refer to the evidence borne by the lexicon to all that the

---

[1] George Smith's *Chaldäische Genesis*, pp. 277 *sq.*
[2] See Baudissin : *Studien zur Semitischen Religionsgeschichte* (1876).

Semites owed to their more civilised predecessors in the way of writing and literature, the ordinary term for "a clay tablet," *duppu*, or *dippu*, for instance, being naturally of Accadian descent; nor need I weary your patience by dwelling any longer on the revelation made by cuneiform research as to the origin of the larger part of Semitic culture. Such a revelation is all the more unexpected, inasmuch as modern scholars, who mostly belong to the Aryan or Semitic families, have been in the habit of assuming that a people who spoke any other than an inflectional language must necessarily be of an inferior type. It is true that China, Mexico, and Peru, or even the Finn, the Magyar, and the Turk of the present day, might be cited against such an assumption; but race prejudices are always strong, and the facts that bear against them are never admitted, except after severe opposition and criticism. Even a philosopher of "common-sense," like Dugald Stewart, once proved to his own and others' satisfaction that Sanskrit was an artificial language invented by the Brahmins to deceive the students of the west; time has shown, however, that the "unphilosophical" and "deluded" students were after all right, and that the critic and his friends were wrong.

But it is not only the origin of Semitic culture that has been revealed by cuneiform research, the nature of the cuneiform system of writing also enables us to discover the degree of civilisation possessed by the Accadians themselves at the time of its invention. Since every character was once a hieroglyphic representing an object or idea, all those objects or ideas which are expressed by simple (and in some cases by compound) ideographs, must necessarily have been known to the inventors of the writing. And further, since the aim of the inventors must have been to give visible representations of all the objects and ideas with which they were acquainted, we may infer that whatever objects or ideas are not so represented must have been unknown to them. Now an examination of the syllabary will lead to the following results. The primitive Accadians were polytheistic, but their worship had already assumed a stellar character quite in accordance with the other indications that we have of the great antiquity of astronomical observations among them. "A deity" is symbolised by a star, "a constellation" by three stars. "The year," too, was already defined, as well as "a month of 30 days;" and an incipient knowledge of mathematics is shown by the existence of ideographs for "number," and "measure." "Law" was administered by the "judge," and "the state" was governed by "a monarch," who received an annual "revenue" from his "subjects." "Slaves" were kept, and the existence of "ships" implies also the existence of sailors. The people dwelt in "houses" of "brick," "wood," and "stone;" these houses were provided with "doors," "beams," and "seats" of wood, and possessed "gardens" in front.[1] A group of houses constituted "a city," which had "walls," "gates," and "a citadel;" the latter, it would seem, was originally built of wood.[2] The cities were connected together by "roads," which crossed one another, and the country was intersected with "canals." It is probable, however, that the characters denoting the latter were added to the syllabary after the Semitic occupation of Shinar, since curiously enough most of the words denoting them (*balag, bulug,*) are of Semitic origin. The temple of the deity resembled an ordinary house; but it contained "a shrine," "an image," and an "altar;" the royal palace was simply "a large house." "Carriages" with "wheels" were used, to which oxen were "yoked." The horse was a subsequent importation from the east, possibly from the Aryan tribes of the Hindu Kush; at all events, its Accadian name was "animal of the east." "Oxen," however, were employed from the first, as well as the ass, which was emphatically termed "the beast," implying that it once held the place afterwards occupied by the horse. The other animals known to the primitive Accadians were "sheep," looked after by "shepherds," "the gazelle," "the antelope," "the bear," "the wild bull," "the dove," "the snake," "the fly," "the flea," "the moth," and some species of "fish." Bees, too, were plentiful, and their "honey" was an article of food. It is plain from this list of animals, that the Accadian hieroglyphics were invented in a mountainous and comparatively cold country.

This agrees with the meaning of the name *Acada*, or "highlander," which is formed from the verb *aca* "to be high," by the individualising suffix *da*, the Assyrian equivalent of "the land of the Accadians" (borrowed afterwards by the Accadians) being *tilla*, or "the heights," from עלה.[3] As I have pointed out

---

[1] That this was the position of the garden or shrubbery is evident from the figure of the character which represented an "enclosure," or "homestead." Even in its Assyrian form ⬛ the fact is shown plainly.

[2] At all events, ⬛, "a fortress" (*manzazu* in Assyrian), was called *gis-gal*, or "great woodwork," in Accadian.

[3] *W. A. I.* II., 48, 13.

on page 43, the earliest writing material seems to have been papyrus rather than the clay of the Babylonian plain, while M. Oppert has noticed that the absence of any simple ideograph for the palm shows that the inventors of the writing must have lived in a colder region than Chaldea. That this colder region was Elam is made evident not only by the name "Accadian," but still more by the fact that the same ideograph, ⏍, denotes indifferently "a country," and "a mountain." Negative evidence also on the same side may be found in the fact, that while "a stream" was represented by a special ideograph, a river was not, an inconceivable occurrence in Babylonia with its two great rivers. So, too, "bitumen," the peculiar product of Chaldea, had no representative in the original collection of ideographs. In fact, the native legends which looked upon the "mountain of the east," the present Elwend, as the peak whereon the ark rested, and the cradle of the Accadian race, contained an element of truth.

Besides the animals already mentioned, the inventors of the cuneiform characters were also acquainted with some kind of cereal, with a sort of "beer," and with the three metals, "gold," "silver," and "bronze." Silver was called "the shining," *babar* (for *barbar*); and the Euphrates in the neighbourhood of Sippara, was entitled the river of "bronze," (*urudu*, Semitised *urudtu*). Only meteoric iron was known, whence it was ideographically denoted by the name of the god Adar. It is noticeable that the vine appears to have been first met with in Babylonia; at all events, it was termed "the tree of life" (*ges-tin*), and not expressed by a simple ideograph. Among precious stones "the diamond" was known, as well as its powers of cutting.

The inventors of the syllabary were armed with "the sword," and "the bow," which was of course accompanied by "the arrow," and "the quiver;" they wore "signet-rings" on their fingers, and "bracelets" on their arms; and dressed themselves in "linen" or "woollen" robes with "sleeves," sometimes dyed "purple," sometimes "variegated;" while their heads were covered with "turbans." They also used "cups" and "buckets," and "papyrus" for writing upon; and their sorcerers prepared various kinds of "poisons." "Witchcraft," indeed, flourished; the national cult was Shamanistic, and it was believed possible to call up the dead. Every object had its "spirit," and "hymns" were composed in honour of the latter. The country contained "marshes" and "jungle," and "the desert" had received a name. The mother occupied the chief place in the family, as is evident not only from an old table of laws given in *W. A. I.* II., 10, and translated by myself in the *Records of the Past*, IV., pp. 21, 22, as well as from the Hymn to the Seven wicked Spirits,[1] where the Accadian order, "female they are not, male they are not," has been reversed by the Semitic scribe, but also from the ordinary Accadian word for "mother," (𒀀𒈠) which appears sometimes as *dagal*, sometimes as *damalla* (i.e., *damála*), or *damal* (*W.A.I.*IV.,9,24,28). Now both *dagal* and *damal* signify "the mistress of the house," being compounds of *dam* "mistress," and *mal* or *gal* "a house." *Mal* is connected with *mal* or *mar* "to dwell," and perhaps also *mar* "a road," (as in *martu* "the west," literally "the path of the setting sun"), *gal* with the verb which signifies "to exist." Both *mal* and *gal*, originally *malla* and *galla*, were in course of time contracted into *mā* and *gā*.

The latter fact is an illustration of the extent to which Accadian came to be affected by phonetic decay, and thus a ready means provided for the transition of an ideograph into the symbol of a syllabic sound. The more I have investigated the phonology of the language the more I have been astonished by the extraordinary extent to which the loss of sounds and syllables was carried. Almost the only parallel I can find to it is in the Mandarin dialect of China; and the literary fossilisation of the language, and the wide spread of education in a country where the very soil furnished materials for supplementing the language of the ear by the language of the eye, had no doubt much to do with this waste and wear of sounds. So also had the contact of the language with the younger and more vigorous Semitic, which tended to enrich itself at the expense of its older neighbour. Final sounds were chiefly attacked, but initial·and even medial letters were also dropped, and it not unfrequently happened that two words of totally different origin came to assume the same form, like our *box* or *sound*. Thus, as noticed above, 𒅗 was primarily a representation of "the tongue" (𒋢), and as such expressed the ideas of "voice," "calling," "assembly," and the like. When inserted within the mouth (𒅗) it denoted sometimes "the tongue," sometimes "speech," sometimes "a nation." Now both these characters originally had the value *eme*, that being the Accadian word which expressed

[1] *W. A. I.* IV., 2, 5, 37, 38.

the ideas they stood for, but in course of time *eme* became attenuated to *me*. On the other hand, there was another word *mes*, (𒈨𒌍) which signified "many," and was expressed by a combination of the two characters 𒈨 (now pronounced *me*) and 𒌍 (*es*). *Mes* often denoted the plural; *mur*, for instance, being "a brick," *mur-mes* (*mür-mös*) "bricks." But with the lapse of time, *mes* was cut down to *me* in Accadian, as in Susianian, where besides the plural affix *mas* or *mes* (*mas* in Protomedic), we find also *me*. Hence it was that 𒈨 "the tongue," came to be employed as the sign of the plural. Another example may be found in 𒃷, originally the representation of a leg or foot (𒑊), which was called *essä* or *essü* in Accadian (Assyrian *sepu*). *Essu* became simple *su*, and the character accordingly passed into a mere allophone of 𒋗 *su* "the hand." The representation of two legs in the act of walking symbolised "going," and its cognate ideas; and the hieroglyphic when laid on its side gave rise to the character 𒁺. Now "to go" in Accadian was denoted by two words, one being *duma*, and the other *ara*. *Duma* became successively *dum*, *dun*, *dŭ*, and *du*, while *ara*, (from which was formed *arig* (*äriga*) "a foot," literally "the goer,") became *ra*. Hence, the use of the character in question with the phonetic powers of *du* and *ra*. Hence, too, its employment in Accadian with *ra*, (𒁺𒁺) in the sense of "going," to signify that it was to be pronounced not *dun*, *du*, or *ara*, but *ra*.

M. Lenormant has shown[1] that the Accadians had classified and named all their characters long before the Semitic conquest of the country. The simple ideographs had been grouped together, like the Chinese "keys" or "radicals," while the compound ideographs were arranged under them and called by appropriate names. Thus 𒅆 was called *igi*, 𒁾 *dib*, 𒊑 *tal*; 𒅆𒁾 being *igidib*, 𒅆𒊑 *igital*. Where the same character was reduplicated, the fact was pointed out by the Accadian word *minnabi* "twice," or its abbreviated form *nabi*: thus 𒈦𒈦 was called *masuminnabi*, or "*masu* twice;" 𒁲 *diliminnabi*, or "*dili* (𒁹) twice." Where the form of a character was changed by the addition of new wedges, the word *gunu* ("tailed" probably), was used; e.g., 𒊓𒄀𒄀 was *saggagunu*, from 𒊓𒄀 *sagga*; 𒊏 was *nindagunu*, from 𒃻 *ninda*. Sometimes *gîtu* "drawn back," or "horizontal," was the epithet employed, as in 𒄿 *i-gîtu*, and 𒊓 *sa-gîtu*. The postposition *cu* "to," occasionally makes its appearance, as in 𒅖𒋻 *gistarurassacu*, "*gistar*

---

[1] In his recent work *Les Syllabaires cunéiformes* (1877).

plus *urassa*," or the 3rd person singular of the aorist of the verb *du* "to go," preceded by the pronoun *gar* "what." Thus ►⊠╪ is called *gar-itu-cu-bat-idu* "what to *itu* (►⊠╪) *bat* (►◄) goes," *i-du* standing for *in-du*. When three characters are united together, the compound ideograph takes its name from all of them; thus ►╪ ►⫡⫡⫡ ⊠►◄⫼⫼ is *gadataccuru*, as being a compound of *gada*, *tak*, and *uru*. The primary object of thus naming the characters was clearly to enable the scribe to write from dictation, and this fact will explain several of the errors met with in the inscriptions. M. Lenormant has pointed out, that in many cases it is only when we refer to the archaic Babylonian form, that the compound character of the ideograph and the reason of its name can be discovered, and since in some few cases even the archaic Babylonian form does not afford an explanation of the name, it is evident that the classification of the syllabary goes back to a very remote period indeed. Many of the so-called syllabaries were drawn up merely for the sake of classifying the characters and cataloguing their names, and they have to be carefully distinguished from those other syllabaries in which the Accadian word in the first column is interpreted by the Assyrian equivalent in the third (or fourth). M. Lenormant has done good service in separating the two kinds of syllabary, and printing them apart. In the case of the first kind, the third column does not contain the Assyrian rendering of the Accadian word in the first, but merely the Semitised form of the Accadian name of the character. Thus *dil* = ► = *dilu*, signifies that the Accadian name of ► was *dil*, to which the Assyrians attached the vowel-ending of their nominative. On the other hand, *di-il* = ► = *na-bu* means that the Accadian word *dil*, represented by the character ►, signified "to proclaim," the Assyrian *nabu*. It may be added that Mr. Smith found a fragment of one of those earlier Babylonian syllabaries of which the Assyrian are but later copies; if the libraries of Babylonia are ever excavated we may expect to discover a complete set.

Before concluding this Lecture, I would draw your attention to the illustration afforded by Assyrian of obscure words and ἅπαξ λεγόμενα in the Old Testament, as well as of words used by Rabbinical authors. I have already alluded to the light thrown by the Assyrian *estin* (or *estinu*) "one," upon the Hebrew *'ashtê* in עַשְׁתֵּי עָשָׂר, another instance would be the ἅπαξ λεγόμενον, אֵבֶה, which occurs in Job ix. 26, and is exactly represented in Assyrian by *abatu*, "a ship." So, too, the Hebrew פֶּחָה and סָגָן, originally applied to Assyrian officers, have received illustration from the Assyrian *pakhat* "a governor," and *sagnu* "a prefect."[1] Naturally Assyrian titles, like those of the Rab-shakeh and the Tartan, have been cleared up. The first denoted the Prime Minister or Grand Vizier, the second the Commander-in-chief of Nineveh. *Rab-shakeh* is the Assyrian *Rab-saki* "great one of the princes," the second part of the compound being of Accadian origin (*sak* "head"); *Tartan* is the Assyrian *Turtannu*, itself derived from the Accadian *Tur-dan*, or "powerful prince." So, again, the meaning of the obscure word אֹחִים in Isa. xiii. 21, translated "doleful creatures" in the Authorised Version, has been determined by the corresponding Assyrian *akhu*, which represents the Accadian *lig-barra* or "hyæna." As might have been expected, many words of rare occurrence in Hebrew are met with plentifully in the inscriptions. I need only refer to *khuratsu*, חרוץ, "gold," *agammu* (*agámu*), אגם, "a pool," or *samullu* (*samúlu*), סמל, "an image."

The language of the Talmud and the Targums was of course largely affected by that of Babylonia. Thus Dr. Delitzsch has pointed out[2] that the Assyrian names of the four winds, *iltanu* or *istanu* "the north," *sûtu* "the south," *sadû* "the east," and *akharru* "the west," are reproduced in the Gemara under the forms of אסתנא, שותא, שדיא, and אוריא. *Sadu* "the east" wind, originally signified the wind of "the mountains," the Accadian *sad*, the mountains in question being those of Elam. *Khazan*, again, in the sense of "governor," explains the חזן of the Mishna, which has now come to mean "a leader" in prayer or singing in the Synagogue. Passing over words like the Assyrian *cissu* (for *cinsu*), "multitude," which corresponds with the Targumic כנש with a שׁ, or the doubling of ר, which was allowed both in Assyrian and Babylonian Hebrew, we find the Assyrian *katu* "a hand," from the Accadian *kat*, reappearing in the Talmudic קתא "a handle." Dr. Neubauer's conjecture that the Talmudic כירי "slave," is derived from כיר "to sell," is confirmed by the Assyrian *kinnatu* "a female slave," which probably goes back to the root קנה "to buy," and, as Harkavy has noticed,

---

[1] Dr. Pusey has observed that the Hebrew טִפְסָר (Jer. li. 27; Nah. iii. 17), translated "captain" in the English Version, is explained by the Accadian *dhip-sar*, "(man of) the written tablet(s)," or "scribe," which was adopted by the Assyrians, and through them handed on to the Jews.

[2] *Assyrische Studien*, i. p. 140.

the Talmudic נדוניא "a gift," finds an explanation in the Assyrian *nadanu* "to give," with ד instead of the usual נתן, while the Targum uses גבב in the sense of "uniting," like the Assyrian *gabbu* "all." A better etymology than the Greek λοῖμος or λιμός can be found for the Rabbinic למס in the Assyrian *lámassu* (*lamásu*) "a colossus," the origin of which is to be sought in the Accadian *lamma* or *lamási*.

The recovery of the Assyrian language, in fact, is vindicating the Semitic nationality of many Targumic and Talmudic words which it has been the fashion to refer to a Greek source. Dr. Delitzsch observes[1] that the Aramaic אַבּוּלָא is not a disguised form of the Greek ἐμβολή, but has its analogue in the Assyrian *abullu* or "city-gate." So, too, קְרִינָא "sweet wine," is connected, not with the Greek κάροινον but with the Assyrian *caranu*, and טכס is to be referred rather to the Assyrian *dhakasu*, "to arrange," than to the Greek τάξις.

But Assyrian lexicography is still in its infancy. We are still employed in completing the grammar of the language, and here alone has anything like success been obtained. An Assyrian grammar is possible, but not yet an Assyrian dictionary. In the preceding course of Lectures I have endeavoured to introduce you to the outlines and main features of that grammar, and to smooth over the difficulties which beset the path of the beginner. How far I may have succeeded is for you to say. In parting, I cannot refrain from thanking you for the attention you have bestowed upon my efforts, and expressing my gratification at the large and persevering group of students that have accompanied me through the dry details of an extinct grammar. Let us not forget that we are all learners together, and that the success which has attended the present course of Lectures is the best possible augury for the future progress and achievements of English Assyriology.

---

[1] George Smith's *Chaldäische Genesis*, p. 298.

For EU product safety concerns, contact us at Calle de José Abascal, 56–1°,
28003 Madrid, Spain or eugpsr@cambridge.org.

www.ingramcontent.com/pod-product-compliance
Ingram Content Group UK Ltd.
Pitfield, Milton Keynes, MK11 3LW, UK
UKHW030902150625
459647UK00021B/2671